I0424177

Redefining Success

Other books by author:

When Mirrors Become Windows, Northwoods Press, Thomaston, Maine, 1985.

Personality and the Soul: Sixteen Women Show Us the Connection, Seven Coin Press, Rockland, Maine, 2001.

Redefining Success

✦

Working Close to Home

Philip C. Groce, MD

iUniverse, Inc.

New York Lincoln Shanghai

Redefining Success
Working Close to Home

Copyright © 2005 by Philip C. Groce

iUniverse books may be ordered through booksellers or by contacting:

iUniverse
2021 Pine Lake Road, Suite 100
Lincoln, NE 68512
www.iuniverse.com
1-800-Authors (1-800-288-4677)

A work of non-fiction written for adults, young and old

Edited by Noreen O'Brien

ISBN-13: 978-0-595-36567-8 (pbk)
ISBN-13: 978-0-595-80997-4 (ebk)
ISBN-10: 0-595-36567-1 (pbk)
ISBN-10: 0-595-80997-9 (ebk)

Printed in the United States of America

To all our neighbors

Contents

Acknowledgements

I thank Dr. Julien S. Murphy, professor of philosophy at University of Southern Maine, for our conversations concerning postmodernism.

Closer to home, I thank Richard and Sheila White for their questions and conversations concerning communities and Dave and Suzy Shaub for their support and input.

I thank Floss Russell for her contribution.

My family helped with this book. They added material and even did some editing. Especially I thank my wife, Dianne, who tolerated my getting up in the middle of the night to write. She also read drafts of all the chapters and told me what she thought. I am a lucky man to have such a family to support me with their love.

Preface

I wrote this book for one purpose, though for me to admit this purpose is sure death with any publisher. I wanted to take a slice out of a well defined community and hold that slice for posterity in order to gauge progress.

One or two hundred years from now, some people will look back at this time and maybe this place and say, "Those were the good old days." I ask the following questions: Are these the good old days in the making? Is there progress? If so, what is progress?

I cannot define progress to anyone's satisfaction, and in reality, satisfaction with ones own life remains the real gauge of progress, and such is a personal definition. True, we can point to medical progress, progress in public health, progress in other sciences, but how does that translate into personal satisfaction?

By reading this book, people of the future will have a gauge of progress, but only by looking at their own lives, knowing how they have faced the same sorts of problems that these people in the book are facing. These people of the future will be able to make a comparison and come away with some gauge of progress as they might define it.

I chose for this book men and women who both live and work in town. That is a special population, but they more than anyone else, are the lifeblood of the town; and they especially enrich it with their efforts. Their battles are not easy battles, and that is why this book has the title that it has. But these same people and their levels of satisfaction are the best gauge of progress for future generations.

Defined communities must survive to promote human satisfaction. Maybe the communities of the future will be virtual communities, I don't know, but I doubt it. Humans are social creatures. Hence I have examined the lives of people who both work and live in a well defined community. Are these the good old days? Or are the better days yet to come? You, of the future, decide.

1

"You gotta know the territory"

I practiced medicine in the small town of Union, Maine, for more than twenty-six years as the only medical doctor. My wife, Dianne, did the office work, and we ran the medical practice from an office in our home where I saw my patients. Over the years, I also made thousands of house calls. I chose to live and work in Union so that I could practice medicine in an atmosphere of trust, and the people of Union have extended that trust in me to write their intimate stories for this book.

One hundred years ago, the men and women of nearly every town both worked and lived in their town. Daily commuting as a concept hardly existed. With the advent of the automobile, people gained independence and began to stretch their horizons and escape from the small factory work, trades work and subsistence farming.

Commuting is now the rule of the day, and people living on the outskirts of a city, known as "bedroom" communities, can enter into that city to do most any kind of work imaginable. Most frequently, people decide to commute because they cannot earn enough money working closer to home. Work life and home life then become two separate universes, and sometimes they become antagonistic.

We will come to see that the decision to live and work in one town accompanies compromises as well as benefits. That decision changes everything. When they opt to work within the community in which they live, men especially find themselves no longer one of many, but one of a few, or more commonly, one alone—peerless. Not very comforting for some, perhaps. We will see how that plays out in the lives of these individuals.

Initially I had intended to write only about men, since my previous book, *Personality and the Soul: Sixteen Women Show Us the Connection*, was about women. After completing this present book, however, I let the concept of it steep in my head for six months and then decided to round out the picture by interviewing wives, partners, associates and sometimes the children involved. Consequently, this book shows the strengths of both men and women.

Individuals who, for instance, choose to work through their computers from a home office are of a different sort than those interviewed for this book. One can work in front of a computer most anywhere, and if the decision is made to do it from home, there may exist conveniences regarding home life, but it remains different from having a business or working within a business in the community in which other community members participate in some way either as customers or as helpers.

We humans are habitual creatures. We feel comfortable in familiar surroundings. We shop in stores we know. We enjoy friends, neighbors and co-workers that we have trusted for years. We surround ourselves with family. In essence, we live in communities. That holds true whether we live in the city, the suburbs or the country.

The community of Union has a rather homogeneous population in class and, with the exception of our family and a few others, race. Look at the community in which you orbit—the people you associate with at work and at home—and you will find a homogeneous collection of individuals—birds of a feather—even though Americans, and especially Mainers, hold pride in their individualism. We will observe how this individualism succeeds in such a small and transparent community.

In the face of so many changes outside ourselves, we humans crave more, not less, of the securities that stable communities offer. At the heart of any community stand the men and women who both live and work there. These people nearly always sacrifice something, usually money in the form of income, in order to live and work in the same community, even if that work is housework and staying at home with the kids. Material wealth and living and working in a community rarely go together.

Communities will not maintain stability unless they have an ability to rule themselves and make their own decisions regarding their form and function. Even though state and federal governments have great influence, the Town of Union, through its town meeting format of government, votes for all appropriations. Every dollar spent by town government earns approval through the vote of the people of Union. Those of us who live in Union take that for granted, but we do so at our own peril.

One person can make a difference. You can know the people in the government. You can see them everyday about town. You will have a hearing if you simply attend selectmen's meetings, though you may not get your way unless you apply a little organizing and political action; but that's the nature of the beast. To preserve the feeling of individual empowerment, the units or atoms of (local) government must remain small. More than anything, the division into smallness will remain the great problem of social engineering for the future. Otherwise, we will become nothing more than a colony of mice.

Something will happen to you after you enter the lives of the people I have brought together in this book, and I will speak to that "something" at the very end.

◆   ◆   ◆

To go any further, "You gotta know the territory," to quote from the opening scene of *The Music Man*, a popular play in Maine. I can watch that play or its movie over and over and always smile at how similar Union is to a small Iowa town before the advent of the automobile. That's true of any well-defined community, not just Union, even though the times have changed. For now, allow me to describe the territory in Union.

Union has a population of about 2,500. It is mostly a rural community, with Route 17, a two-lane highway, bypassing the village center and connecting Camden and Rockland on the coast to Augusta in the epicenter of the state. Entering the township on Route 17, there are farms with cows or sheep grazing the hills, in the distance, a steeple or two piercing the sky from the village center. There is the Come Spring Diner, with patrons' pickup trucks parked out front, several convenience stores and a handful of other businesses, all holding on as best they can, because the large "box" stores, Wal-Mart and Home Depot, have recently appeared on the coast, sixteen miles east of Union.

Union hasn't grown much in population over the years, and before the advent of the automobile, it remained stable with a carriage industry, a casket factory, apple and blueberry packing, barrel stave fabrication and the sale of limestone from several quarries. A short canal and a standard gauge railway carried the produce of these industries to the main rail line along the coast. Water now fills all the limestone quarries, and though signs prohibit swimming, passing motorists might catch glimpses of teenagers taking advantage of the summer sun lounging on the quarries' steep edges, or passersby on foot might hear an occasional splash as the divers hit the water. The older the photo, the more cleared land is evident throughout Union. A great deal of that agricultural land has grown up into forest or has been sliced into house lots, though a large housing development in Union would be ten houses, not 500.

In the early spring or fall, the air holds hints of the smell of grass burning from the blueberry fields—each field burned every other year to prune the berries and clear the weeds. Motorists might catch the smell of skunk in the air, killed the night before on the road, or perhaps see blood splashed on the highway from deer hits. Stains remain on the road a year or two before weather and traffic erase them. When the trucks aren't rumbling along Route 17, crows can be seen rummaging for a meal in the fields, or a flock of passing geese honking overhead can be heard. On the secondary roads of the town, walkers, while swatting at black flies along their chosen route, will hear loons yodeling from the nearby lakes.

The focus of this book is the village center, the heart of Union. I will lead you on a ten-minute walk up from Sunk Haze, a low area next to the St. George River and, continuing through the Common, make a right turn at the post office. From there, we will go down a hill, passing older residences along the way, to the bottom of the hill at the blueberry packing plant on our left. When we reach the cemetery at the top of the next hill, which is beyond the village proper, we will have encountered nearly all of those interviewed for this book. Those interviewees not living or working on this path, I chose because of their connection to the people along that path.

On our walk through the Common, we will pass a couple of stores, a hairdresser and barber shop, a bank, a restaurant, a bed and breakfast, the town library/historical society and a vacant lot where there once was a Laundromat and a chiropractor's office, but that old wooden building burned in a spectacular fire in 2002. Townspeople stood on the Common and watched the volunteer fire departments from several towns expertly contain the blaze, which threatened to engulf the adjoining buildings. Close enough to feel the intense heat of the blaze we all participated by watching.

On the Common, with its well-shorn grass and shady maple trees, we find a gazebo or bandstand and the essential Civil War statue. There's a painted road sign denoting the mileage to various places and a map with the location of historical sites in Union. On one edge of the Common sits the only restaurant that serves beer and wine—there are no liquor sales in Union.

Town government is through a town manager, but five elected selectmen hold the power. Some of selectmen are women, though no one uses the term "selectwomen," and selectpersons sounds too weird for anyone to use. The selectmen earn $600 a year for attending biweekly meetings and public hearings, not to mention all the telephone calls from upset townspeople made just as these individuals are sitting down to supper at home. The Town meets each year to vote on the entire budget, and the selectmen can call special town meetings for important matters. Some meetings attract so many attendees the meetings are held in the firehouse. Other public meetings have only a few attending. Democracy in Union, as in all small Maine towns, remains as direct as democracy can be, and the townspeople elect nearly all the officials, such as members of the budget committee and the school board.

Ah, the school board. Members rarely last a full term. Considerable time is required just to find an individual willing to file the papers to run for a position on this board. Usually, a newcomer not "in the know" will run after a longtime resident has talked him or her into this thankless job. Some are exceptions—my wife, born and bred in Maine—was one of the exceptions. She completed a three-year term, despite the grumblings of her husband.

There is one public school in town, the International School, holding kindergarten through grade eight. Remarkably, each class studies a different country every year. The high school, however, is regional, but not so very long ago it, too, was local. What was then the school is now a community center—Thompson Community Center—named after Dr. Augustin Thompson, inventor of the carbonated drink, Moxie. When he was alive, Dr. Thompson lived up the road from where I live. A rugged few still drink Moxie. In the absence of supporting evidence, Dr. Thompson eventually withdrew the claim that Moxie had health benefits, and the young man wearing a white coat and holding forth a bottle of Moxie disappeared from the advertisements, replaced by young, beautiful women.

The hills, with the ancient glacial valleys and many small lakes, produce microclimates throughout the town, though the weather generally can be characterized by one word—changeable. Living in Maine, one becomes accustomed to noticing the direction of the wind: southwesterly with warm moisture and the faint hint of Midwest ozone, northwesterly with the crispness of Canada, northeasterly with the smell of the ocean and rain or snow splattering one's face, and the tropical gales, and sometimes hurricanes, from the southeast.

All in all, it's our town, foul weather, blackflies and all, and you are about to examine its innards.

2

Adventureland

I begin on the edge of the Common next to Mark Hannibal's restaurant, Hannibal's Café. One now has a view of the St. George River, because the Laundromat next door burned two years ago. This is the same view Mark has from his living space on the second floor above the restaurant. Mark is remembered for futilely spraying a garden house on the blazing old wooden Laundromat before the fire departments arrived, after which he began hauling important documents and memorabilia out of his own building. Neighbors were helping, but as it turned out, the side of Mark's restaurant was only roasted, not burned.

I begin at Mark's while sitting at the counter in his restaurant with my wife. We were having a chicken quesadilla chased by several brews one lazy summer afternoon. I engaged in conversation a man at a nearby table who lives on the other side of Union and who makes musical instruments. Sitting with his wife and young family, the man was roughly dressed, and had his hair pulled back in a ponytail. While we were chatting, Mark, in his white chef's outfit, walked to the counter from the kitchen and joined the conversation. I don't remember what we talked about, but it occurred to me that we four (my wife included) had a line of commonality, that we each lived and worked in Union.

I thought about others who live and work within the town, and I knew that I could walk down the road by the Common and encounter many of them one by one. Days later and after much more thought, I decided to interview Mark. Later, I would go to Frank Austin's just off the Common in Sunk Haze and begin a walk through the Common and beyond, interviewing the people as they appear along the path.

I chose to take just one path through the town, because I still have to live here, and I don't want people coming up to me saying, "Why didn't you interview so-and-so?" knowing that they really meant to ask why had I not interviewed them rather than so-and-so. My response will be to ask how much more scientific could I be if I am simply taking the individuals as they come along the one path.

That is actually more random than me selecting, cherry picking style, whomever I wanted throughout the town. In retrospect, this plan worked out best.

Is this science? Ha to that. I have my own way of looking at things. So do the people with whom I have talked. Tell me about science and human behavior and human choices, and you might as well throw logic right out the window. A good place for it. Regardless, something meaningful is happening here, and we are going to discover as much of it as we can.

◆　　　◆　　　◆

Until the time of Mark's interview, I hadn't realized that Mark was from San Diego and that he attended a high school not far from the one I attended. Hannibal's Cafe serves classy, offbeat food in a pleasant environment. Family and friends sit for hours talking after a meal.

With his surfer-shaped body, his closely shorn blonde hair, round wire rim glasses, small goatee under his lower lip, though pushing mid-forties, Mark looks like a California boy, but the telltale evidence is his casual speech. That indescribable something that makes people around here say that you can take the boy out of California, but you can't take California out of the boy. Mark is divorced and sharing custody of his three boys, the oldest being fifteen, in his apartment over the restaurant.

"Why did you leave San Diego?" I asked him.

"When I got out of high school, I was frustrated by the lack of changing seasons, and I was pretty much dissatisfied with who had the best car, the best girlfriend—and all the partying, the superficiality."

"Do you miss anything about it?"

"The beaches, the weather, the availability of stuff like Mexican food. Just the ethnic diversity—the languages, the writing on signs that you can't understand, but you know that somebody understands it. That must have some effect."

"What effect?" I asked.

"That *other things* are going on outside of what you do."

"Where did you go after California?"

"I went to Oregon and lived on communes for four years."

"What kind of an experience was that?"

"The first was an 'intentional' community—intent on being based on Krishnamurti's teachings. I lived there for a while, then I met a guy who had bought five acres from the commune. He was a sociology professor. I ended up caretaking his property neighboring the commune and working in a Mexican restaurant, too. The property became an 'unintentional' community, and more of a community than the commune across the creek, the one based on Krishnamurti."

"How was that?

"We joked about it—all their power struggles. The commune across the creek had a board of directors made up of the people who started it in the first place, and many of them then lived in San Francisco, making big bucks."

"The commune was sort of like having a vineyard?" I interjected.

"Yeah." Mark sort of laughed. "We did some good things on our side of the creek. Each of us had our own little houses and gardens. We built things together, and each Sunday we met to decide who would help cook the daily meal. You could eat at your own house, too. It was sort of like living in the community of Union. We have communal stuff that goes on right in this restaurant: wedding meals, funeral get-togethers. A lot of people meet here. We've even had a few proposals of marriage."

"What did you come away with, having lived in a commune?"

"I expanded what I mean by community, and it certainly doesn't require that you have bare feet, be all of the same political bent, eat only organic food and go around unwashed. In a community, you provide for yourself, and when you do that, you enrich the entire community. You need enough diversity to keep it going. The strength is in diversity."

"What do you mean by 'diversity'?"

He thought for a moment. "Diversity is anything that, say, I didn't happen to think of—something I don't particularly believe in, but I'm ready to compromise and make room for it. If I'm not giving up preconceptions, then I'm not giving up anything."

Diversity of ideas, I thought to myself. I like that angle on diversity. "Preconceptions are prejudices," I said.

He nodded. "You have to take risks, have to move ahead with the faith that there's a more powerful element at play."

"For instance?"

"I've developed a broader spiritual awareness. I have a friend who is a pastor. I gave him some Buddhist material that I read, and I told him that it looks similar to the Christian stuff. So maybe Christ, when he was away for a time, visited them over there and hung out with those guys, but nobody would listen to them, but they did to Him."

"Why did you leave the commune?"

"I was getting bored. We were in a very rural area. I wanted to travel, maybe go to school. My mom had moved to Maine with her new husband. I thought I would go there, check it out, have an adventure."

"Did you go to Maine directly?"

"I'm a goal-oriented, focused guy, so I beat feet over there. I didn't hang out anywhere along the way. I guess I should have."

"Being as goal-oriented as you are, was it frustrating to deal with others in the commune, many of whom may not have been as goal-directed as you?"

"Yeah. Some of them were getting food stamps. They could've worked."

"Were you always so goal-oriented? Perhaps ambitious is a better word."

"As a kid I used to go door-to-door with a stencil, and I would paint the house numbers on the curb to earn money. I mowed lawns—whatever. I figure that you *have* to provide for yourself. If not, then someone else has to provide for you."

"Not everyone has that much self-reliance," I said.

"I know," he replied. "That's why our taxes are so high. I don't mind helping people—that's our responsibility in a community—to help others. But I don't want to do it if they can do it for themselves. I've fired a number of people who don't want to work—shuffling their feet—they're more efficient in work-avoidance, and they're good at it, crafty enough to find ways around work, trying to work it so everyone else ends up doing the job for them. I see them in the grocery store with food stamps. Unemployment insurance, I mean, is there for a reason. I feel the responsibility to help when there isn't enough work, but people get unemployment even when I have work for them here. They just don't want to do it."

"Do you think it's any different finding good employees in Maine compared to elsewhere?"

"No, it's the same. Some people haven't had the role models in life, and that's the way they think the world is supposed to work. I try to teach my employees integrity in their job, to feel good about doing their best. I reamed a kid out just the other day, because I know he's a pothead. He doesn't come to work high, but I know that he smokes every day. Even if he isn't high, it still affects his performance. Here I'm watching the result of his pot use, and I pull him aside, and I say to him, 'Now you're going to say that I'm such an old dude, but I have enough experience to know what's going on with you. I refuse to believe that you're just stupid, because I know you're not.'"

I interrupted Mark. "What kind of bad results are you talking about?" With that question, a smile appeared on Mark's face. I asked him, "What are you smiling about?"

"This is kinda funny," he said. "And it really happened. This guy comes into the restaurant and wants a cup of coffee. So the kid gets him the coffee from the air pot—these Thermos containers we use to hold the hot coffee. The customer calls the kid over and says that the coffee isn't hot enough and maybe he could heat it up in the microwave. The kid takes the cup away, and he's gone for a while. He comes back and tells the customer that he's sorry but he can't heat up the coffee.

"Then the customer asks, 'Why not?' And the kid says, 'Because the air pot is too big to fit in the microwave.'"

We both laughed.

"That really happened," said Mark. "I mean, some of these kids can't remember one week to the next what I'm trying to teach them. I try to point out some of this stuff that's going on to my *own* kids, for education. There's sex education, too." He glanced at me.

"What do you mean?"

"This one employee got his girlfriend pregnant, and he told me that he was going out West to experience some adventure. He said he had plans. 'Yeah,' I said to him, 'You're going to have plans to rent the apartment over the video store. That's going to be your big adventure.' I make certain my own kids are taking this all in."

"If you try to educate your employees, do they then move on?"

"Not always. Some people appreciate being shown how to work, or they already know. Here they can learn a craft they can take anywhere."

"How does one go about teaching responsibility?"

"I was just thinking about that with my own kids. If they spill something, I show them where the towel is and how to clean it up. I say that I understand that it was an accident, but everyone has a function in the family—like spokes on a wheel. They don't innately know that. That's our job as parents to show them. They come into this world getting fed, clothed and cleaned up after. Then they try to play that out as long as they can."

"What happened after you arrived in Maine?"

"I worked in restaurants along the coast. Then I saw an ad for a chef's school. I figured that I had been wanting to go to school, and I already had ten years or so in restaurant work. So, I went to the Culinary Institute of America in New York for two years. I met Liz before I went, and we got married before I finished, and she got pregnant. I hadn't come to Maine to be here the rest of my life. I was a fresh graduate, and I could go anywhere in the U.S. and get a good job. My wife didn't want to leave Maine, so I took a job at an upscale restaurant on the coast.

The chef I worked for was a mentor for me. He had been doing it his whole life. It was a great job, and I stayed four years—paying rent, then buying a house. Then we had another kid. It was getting harder and harder to even think about leaving."

"Do you have a fantasy about an ideal life and job?" I asked.

"I always figured I'd have a family and settle down, but when I came to Maine, I thought I was going on an adventure, and then I'd return to Oregon, because I sort of found myself there."

"What did you expect in Maine?"

"When I was in Oregon, I thought Maine was going to be like the North Pole. You'd be surprised. A lot of people in Oregon didn't even know where Maine is. They would ask me why I wanted to go there, and I would tell them I wanted to have an adventure. I never thought it would stop right here."

"How did you come about starting your own shop?"

"Since I was nineteen, I knew that I could run my own place. When I was working for the guy on the coast, I began to see how things could be done better. The guy would tell me that he does things in a particular way, because it's his place. That's the way it is.

"I had pretty clear ideas of what would work. I never really gave up the idea of living communally, but things just didn't turn out the way I thought. Do you know that the hippie-types are the hardest to wait on in a restaurant?"

I shook my head.

"Well they *are*. They snap their fingers and expect people to fall all over them: 'Where's my coffee, dude? Just because I smell bad and I have dreadlocks, why don't I get service like anyone else?' I mean, what is this, some kind of crusade? I've found that a lot of those people have chips on their shoulders."

He looked at me. I didn't know what to say. Then he exhaled, paused and continued, "I guess I wasn't much different. When I was in Oregon, I wore a skirt—a goddamned skirt—when I did my laundry in town, a logging town, no less. I had a beard then. So I guess I can understand people trying to shake things up—I did—but when it comes to being rude—there's no call for being rude."

"Why did you choose Union?"

"We were living in Hope, inland, near Union. Working on the coast didn't make any sense. I mean, there was a store out here in Union, a bank, a community, and it seemed that there needed a good place to eat, too. People get sick of driving to the coast. Now we draw people to the restaurant from all over, but when we first opened, we were flying on a hope and a prayer with very little cash, and less of a credit line. We opened without even an adequate exhaust fan. The first night, grilled salmon filled the place with smoke, and I had to open the door—something I didn't plan on. It was cold outside. Later on, we did have some help from Liz's parents. They wanted to see us succeed, but they didn't want to do it for us."

Liz and Mark had rented the lower half of the building containing the Laundromat. Later, they bought the boarding home next door, since the boarding home went out of business. They remodeled it with the restaurant below, and the apartment above.

"In the old building, it was funky," I said. I didn't tell him that I liked funky, that I could put my feet up on the chairs, as I do at home. I guess you might call that slouch, not funk.

"It *was* funky," he said, "but I didn't intend that. I started with what I had, with what money I had. I remember writing the specials on the wall—they were made of abitibi, and you could erase it. Some of the chairs had tears [probably because *some* customers felt comfortable enough in the restaurant to put their feet on them], but now I have better chairs. Still, there's stuff I'm not happy with. I'd like to have nicer, more comfortable chairs. As I mature, my tastes change, and I'm less likely to put up with crude stuff. I've been in business now for ten years. Hard to believe!"

"Now that you have your own place, how do you respond if one of your employees wants to do something his or her own way?"

"There's more than one way to skin a cat, but it's my name over the door. I will try to see if the idea works by doing it their way, and if it doesn't, then I go back to my way. For instance, I want to give the customers water as soon as they sit down. In some places, they have to ask for it. It's my place, and I have the right to make that choice."

"Is it difficult to get good help?"

"I have people here who have worked with me for years. Others try it and find right off that it's not for them. It's a small place—nowhere to hide—some are more comfortable in a bigger place. All restaurants get used to a transient work force. I don't have enough hours to offer as a career job for a chef—that's what I do, myself. I take a lot of people who haven't had a job before, and I teach them about restaurants. If they can know their way around a kitchen, then they can get a job just about anywhere. For instance, I have a new kid who never worked before. I had to tell him that this is *not* a school project. Once he punches the time clock then he has to turn on to what he can do to help this place. I show him what he can do."

"How often are you pleasantly surprised that an employee will pick up the ball?"

"Most people need management, and only a few will become their own boss, no matter what age. I tell them, even if it's the dish space, 'You rule this area, and as long as you do your job, you won't be hearing much from me, until it's time to learn new stuff and earn more.' Who wants a boss breathing down your neck? As a boss, though, I can't give up. I have to keep at it all the time—like with raising kids. It's my job. It's a matter of pride. When a customer goes to the restroom and he happens to look into the kitchen, I want him to see that even the dish room looks good."

"So it takes self reliance and self-directedness to do what you do, and you, in turn must try to infuse those qualities into your own employees in order to succeed."

"Exactly. I tell them that this is something to learn, and not just for this job, but for the next and the next. You want me to give the recommendation to your next employer that you would be a good addition to the crew. The more you learn, the more you earn. Even if you do the dishes, if you do each dish, but there's no enthusiasm, then you'll be here only until someone with enthusiasm comes along."

"You must have a high turnover," I said.

"I do," he admitted, "but this year, recently in fact, three past employees came back after being gone, one for five years, to see if I had work for them. One was a totally different person, and he's now planning to go to the Culinary Institute just like I did. So, I must be doing something right. I know I'm not exactly a pushover. One of the workers said to me, 'When you get mad, I'm scared, dude, even when you're not even talking to me.'"

"How do you pick a new employee?"

"I go by my feelings, but I always check references. I had one kid—he had [body] piercing all over the place—I checked his references, and they said he was trouble, that he stole on the job. But I got good vibes from him. I thought that he could be good, and I told him the situation; that people were telling me not to hire him, but that this was an opportunity, and if he would give me his word to work all summer, I would give him a good recommendation. Well, he was awesome. He calls me every couple of years to tell me about the famous chefs he's working with now."

"What can you say to a person who applies for work at your place, and may also be applying to, say, MBNA. Why should he or she work for you?" [The credit card giant, MBNA, has in recent years moved into Maine along the coast with its telemarketing division.]

"It's a smaller environment here. It's in the community, more intimate." He thought for a few moments. "It's not just about money. It's the same reason that I went into this business in the first place. I didn't do it for the money—it's an art form—an art form that I do well. It's feeding people and part of the entertainment business—they call it the hospitality industry—to have the notion of making people feel good; from a great cup of coffee served at just the right time, or eggs Benedict that look great and taste even better. Food is a powerful media, and being there and providing it can be very rewarding. Where is the art at MBNA—coaxing people to go into debt?"

"Doesn't your brother work for MBNA?"

"We would have arguments. He told me that I wouldn't have such a problem keeping good employees if I offered benefits like he's getting. I can offer benefits, but I told him that MBNA has the entire world as a market. I only have this little area. But, you know, he doesn't work for MBNA anymore, and I have another person here that used to work at MBNA.

"We're talking about feeding people. A meal is immediate, and it can effect how you feel. You can share it; it's sensory; it has taste, smell and you read about it on a cold piece of paper, and then it comes to you in 3-D. When people come in, they will have a positive experience and not just empty calories. Not everything is particularly healthy, but it's well-crafted food, and you'll feel good eating it. I give the option of lighter food. I like feeding people. I had some meals when I was growing up that I remember to this day—when the food gets into your mouth and everything stops. It's the most incredible thing—everything else *stops*. I want people, when they get ready to leave, to think that we were so nice and helpful. They could say, 'Maybe I like my steak done in a very particular way, and maybe I'm an impossible customer, but these people really tried.'"

The phone rang. Mark answered it, talked briefly then returned. "That was my girlfriend," he said, hiding a smile. "Well, we're engaged. She's at USM [University of Southern Maine], and she plays basketball, a star player. She's pretty high profile, and my life's pretty public; so when she's not at school, we'd just as soon lay low. When she's away at school, the cell phones rule."

I remember seeing his girlfriend work in the restaurant the last two summers. She's tall, blonde and very pretty.

"Returning to what we were talking about. Your answer to the person applying for work at both your place and MBNA is that you are trying to do an art form, is that accurate?"

"Yes. What I'm doing is an enriching experiencing—like good the-ater—things enriching to your soul and your being."

"Are you able to get that across to your employees?"

"Those who don't share that philosophy don't stay. Many people who work in restaurants are in it for themselves, and they screw other workers out of side work, steal. This is such a small place. They can't tolerate the closeness."

"What do you do when you get fed up with it all?"

"I blow off steam, maybe bitch about people who don't want to wait fifteen minutes for a table, when they don't complain about doing the same thing at Moody's [Maine's famous diner in Waldoboro]. They wait forty-five minutes at Olive Garden, and they get one of these little buzzers, and here you could have a cup of coffee on the veranda, but they wig out."

"Why stay in Union?"

"I had a consultant and he listened to my philosophy, looked at my books, looked at the community. He said that if I wanted to make money, I should move onto Route 17—buy Elmer's old place [previously a restaurant] before the insurance company bought it. An accountant type, he was only interested in the bottom line."

"Why didn't you do it?"

"It just wasn't me. This way, it's efficient. I live upstairs. I can walk to the gro-cery store, to the bank, the post office. It's as if people are coming to my own house to eat. A long time ago, people used to work near or where they lived. This living in one place and working in another is a new concept as far as human his-tory is concerned. It's more natural, I think, to live where you work. I can spend more time with my family—hang out with my boys when business is slow, skate-board or sled out back with them, help with homework, whatever. It's easier to find a new job than a new family, and with kids you only get one shot at it; after eighteen years or so, they move on.

"Working outside of where you live is like trying to find fulfillment—outside of yourself. Living here has its downside, too—less privacy, less money. Living in this community is much the same as this job. Some do more; some do less, but it's become a type of family. I know I don't have enough seats in this place to get rich, but I love what I do, and it's working for my family and me. What more do I need?"

The phone rang. It was his fiancé again, and I knew that it was time for me to leave.

◆   ◆   ◆

Since Mark had so much to say about his employees, I decided to talk to one of them, Rich Wiemer. Rich marched in the graduation procession nearly two years ago at the high school gym, in the same line as our oldest son, Paul. Rich's parents sat together in the bleachers, smiling.

Rich now works in the kitchen with Mark, where I tracked him down because he's rarely home. At the time of this interview, Rich was paying rent at his father's house, but he has since rented a house in town along with several other guys. Since his parents' divorce, Rich's mother has lived in a new house next door to his father's, with Rich's younger sister.

I asked Rich for an interview as he was coming into the restaurant's kitchen from the storeroom. I saw a look that was half his mother's look of questioning, and half of Mark's "This is my territory" look. He seemed taller than I remembered him while we stood in the kitchen, or maybe, as with our house, the floor sagged where I was standing. Or maybe he's now a man and I remember him as a boy when he played in the tree in our dooryard with Paul. He's fair, like Mark, and he has the face of a beautiful baby grown up. As my wife says, "He's cute, and I love him." I never remembered him looking me in the eye when I talked with him before, but now, he seemed solid. Later, we sat at the kitchen table at my house for the interview.

"Rich, what were you thinking as you were marching in the graduation line at Medomak [High School]?"

"I was scared to death," he replied without hesitation. "For a couple of months, it looked pretty bleak that I would even be there. I had no idea what I was going to do. I had done nothing about college, and I didn't know where I was going. I figured it was pointless to pay more money for more schooling."

"Sounds like graduation was a non-event," I said.

He sighed. "Not really, but my friends were going off to school, and into subjects I couldn't even understand what they *were*, and I was working at the Samoset [a resort in Rockland] full-time. I was sort of jealous. I knew I could have done better."

"What were you doing at the Samoset?"

"Bussing tables."

"You had worked for Mark before?"

"Yeah, when I was fifteen—dishwashing and some prep work."

"What was that like?"

"Just a job. I hated it, but I had to work to make ends meet, to pay for a car. I worked for a year. He wasn't very nice, I thought, but I don't really think it was him. I was only fifteen, and he had a business to run. I guess I was a little punk."

"How did things end then?"

"He called me in and said that it seemed I wasn't happy to be there; so why come in? So I didn't, and business was slowing down for the winter, anyway."

"Then you worked at the Samoset. School was still going on. How did that work out?"

"I hated every day of it. I didn't like bussing. I wanted to work in the kitchen. After about a year, I got the chance to work in the Club House Grill, cooking mostly hamburgers. Things changed, and I had a blast. I enjoyed learning from the chefs. They were kids like me, only a little older, but I could look up to them."

"Do you think it was your age—a little older than when you worked at Mark's—that allowed you to look to role models at the Samoset, because it sounds as if you refused to listen to Mark."

"Mark was going through the 'Liz thing' [Mark's ex-wife]. He wasn't a very warm character—unsatisfactory as a role model."

"You had your parents. They're pro-education, both professionals."

"I didn't like any of that stuff. I decided that I was going to find *my* thing."

"So you continued at the Samoset?"

"After the Grill, they let me into the kitchen—line cooking, banquets. It was coming on easy. I enjoyed kitchens, where everyone could be themselves, not kissing up to the people in the dining room. I could be proud of my work. I decided that I wanted to be a chef."

"Can you remember when you made that exact decision?"

"I was out behind the grill on a cigarette break, by myself. I had been thinking for a long time about what I would do with my life. I remembered that my parents used to say that if you don't like going to work, then you're in the wrong field. I couldn't go wrong with that choice."

"What do you think pushed you into that decision on that particular day?"

"I figured it was time for me to buckle down. I had seen my friends go off. I had to find where I was going and stop doing so much partying around town. I wasn't going to be like the guy I know who lives down on Wotton Mill Road and has never been anywhere and never intends to leave the place."

"What is your vision for your future?"

"Long term, I don't really know, but I want to go to cooking school, get out of the state of Maine for a while."

"Do you think you would ever return to Maine?"

"Oh, I would come back to Union. Union's awesome. People here are so much different; they're nice, not like they are, say, in Connecticut. I want the freedom to go out in my backyard, walk around and not run into another house."

"Do you see things in work that, if you were the boss, you would change?"

"Some of it is just simple renovations, but in the food perspective, I'm still trying to learn. I do think that with some of the younger employees I wouldn't have such a short fuse. Better to work things out, rather than say that if you don't want this job, I'll find someone that does. You got to realize that when a new person comes online, everything drops off for a while. It takes time for things to smooth out."

"If you had the last four or five years to live over again, what would you do differently?"

"I would have paid attention to high school. Now I'm applying to school, and they want SAT scores. I would have listened to the teachers and other adults."

"Irrespective of you having to prove yourself to other schools now, do you think that if you paid more attention in school, when you were in school, that it would be of value to you now in your everyday life and in your work?"

He thought for a moment. "No, it doesn't apply to my life. That's a good question."

"You could have received culinary arts training in the vocational school at Medomak. Did you make that choice?"

"How could I? I had no idea that I wanted to be a chef, and I wouldn't have known it if I didn't go off to do what I did. All I knew was that I didn't like working for Mark in the kitchen. Taking chemistry, biology, and Spanish—all of which I hated—certainly didn't help me."

"The fact is that you are in school now, learning at the restaurant."

"It's a different kind of education," he said. "School felt like a prison, but I could have been a lot more productive in school. I was worried about the social thing. It was so important."

"Where does your social life fit into your life now?"

"I don't really socialize much anymore. My friends are either off to college or they're in Boca."

"You're talking about the group of guys from here that work in the resorts in Florida during the winter?"

"Yeah. I couldn't do that—folding laundry, making money, getting drunk. All that doesn't excite me much."

"What is it like when they come home and you see them?"

"They think highly of themselves, saying, 'I'm the man.' I thought that when you went away you were supposed to change for the better. They have no idea what they want to do."

"What's it like working in the kitchen?"

"I like the gang. I learn something new everyday. I try to think of how I would do things differently."

"What do you do for fun in the kitchen, the stuff behind the scenes?"

"It's not like that TV show where it's a big social thing. It's more screwing around, making it fun to work. We dare each other. Yesterday we dared one of the dishwashers to chug-a-lug a whole pint of Worcestershire sauce without stopping, for $5—the *whole* pint."

"Did he do it?"

"Sure did. It almost made me vomit watching him—that stuff is really rank."

"How about him?"

"He almost puked. He looked pale. Last week, for $10 we dared him to lick his tongue all the way across the floor of the kitchen, maybe twenty feet."

"That's awful. What happened?"

"He did it, and you should have seen his tongue—it was all dark."

"Was he desperate for the money?"

"No, I don't think it was the money. More because of the bet."

"Do you have bad days in the kitchen?"

"Maybe if I didn't get enough sleep, or if I'm having girlfriend troubles."

"Does work make you modify your outside life in any way?"

"Yeah, sure. It's forcing me into regulating my life so I can do better at work. When I first started working this time around, I smoked a lot of pot, then Mark pulled me aside and said, 'Dude, you got to lay off the pipe. It really affects you, your memory. It makes a big difference.' So I thought I'd give it a try, and if it helps, I'd do it. And he was right—especially about motivation."

"I think other kids might listen to you."

"If I'm going to share my life's experiences with them, I would need to be older."

"Where do your parents fit into this equation?"

"My parents are behind me, but they wish I was in school. Next year my sister is going to be in high school. I can see that they're really beginning to crack down on her. I don't think she's ready for it. These girls, they want to grow up so fast."

"What do you think of the way you were raised?"

"I think it could have been better. Most of it's trial and error, anyway, but the more I see of what other kids have had to go through, the better my life seems. I was a difficult kid, a brat. I think it was best when they made me work for what I got, not just gave me things."

"How would you have handled you, if you were they?"

"Some of the stuff that was said—I wouldn't have done that. I would have tried to listen a bit more—maybe slap me around a bit."

"Your parents divorced when you were a junior. But they continued to live next door to one another. What was that like?"

"I was fortunate, because when I talk to my friends, their parents' divorces sound pretty rough. It was kinda awkward explaining it to people, but I was lucky, because, say, if I got hungry, I could just walk over to my mom's house and get something to eat."

"Did you have the best of both worlds?"

"Not really—well, maybe. Yeah, I guess I did."

"I don't want to put words in your mouth."

"I think I did, really."

"Mark says that serving food to people is an enriching experience, like good theater, good for the soul and one's being. Are you into food in that way?"

"People come in to relax and to eat. I never looked at it in that way. It's kind of interesting, though."

"When I first asked you that question, I saw a look on your face, and I thought perhaps your first thought was that it was bullshit."

"No, that's not true, but maybe I'll feel like he does when I'm older."

"How important is money to you?"

"I want to be secure, not to have to hustle to pay bills."

"In Maine?"

"I think I could find the right place, the right people. Mark could make a lot of money in Camden. He could be charging an extra $4 on a piece of meat there. They'd pay it."

"Do you look forward to the future?"

"It's definitely an adventure. Everyday is different in the kitchen—never had the same thing happen twice."

"I can find cooking at home tedious, what with the dishes, the mess," I said.

"Cooking in a restaurant is different from that. You have everything prepped, and you can just do it. You give the dishes to the dishwasher. I hate cooking at home."

I didn't tell Rich that when I walked into the restaurant that afternoon, before he arrived to work, I saw Mark washing dishes with a not-so-happy look on his face. Ah, the adventure of ownership.

◆   ◆   ◆

Mark lives in the same building in which he works. I can identify with his situation and approach as I had the medical practice in my home in Union for many years. I will tell you some of my own experience, and you can see there are broad parallels in our work lives, not to mention our origins—both of us being immigrants to Maine from California.

In our old Victorian farmhouse, we had only one bathroom, which was okay, because it was just off the examining room, which was the dining room originally. When the children were younger, occasionally they would have to come through the examining room during office hours to use the bathroom. Other times, they could use the outhouse in the barn.

By the time we had four children, we had to add a bathroom upstairs, but all during this time, the children knew that we, their parents, were around, because my wife was my only help in the office. I worked with no nurse, and when it came time to pay, I personally presented the bill to my patients.

While I am not using myself as any sort of model, I do know that by living and working within the same community, I was able to keep a finger on the pulse of my work. Physicians today must practice so-called "defensive medicine," tending to have patients return for rechecks. Ordinarily, I did not do that, and I left it to the patients to return if they thought a recheck was needed, or I would ask them to telephone to let us know how they were doing. That, in itself, cut down on unnecessary office visits and saved the patients money in the process.

I knew that either my wife or I would be in town, at the store, or at the post office, and we were kept informed of what was going on in the community. People would sidle up to me saying, "By the way, Doc…" If my wife went to the store in Union, even if she said that she was only going to take a few minutes to get milk, we knew it was going to take a lot longer than that. People liked talking to her since she has a much friendlier personality than I have, and they knew she would relay important information.

Physicians in particular wonder if such a practice has a risky side. I can only say that I never had a lawsuit for anything, or even a threat of one. I wanted to practice medicine only in an atmosphere of trust. It probably helps to make house calls, too. When I first arrived in Maine, an older physician, Richard Waterman, wanted me to work with him in another town. While he was showing me around in his car, he was naming off the diseases in each house as we cruised down a country road in Waldoboro. I thought I would never end up like that;

however, that is precisely what I did do. Dr. Waterman is long retired now. I took over his practice for a couple of weeks when I first arrived, and that gave him his first vacation in years. To a great degree, I copied his style of practice. Now I can go down the road and name off the diseases, too.

Because I hate schedules, and I especially hate future commitments, throughout the twenty-six years of my office practice I would not make appointments more than a week in advance (I note that Mark does not accept reservations at his restaurant). When someone wanted to be seen, all they had to do was call, and they could be seen that day, or perhaps the next. Some people would just drop by for an office visit during the time that they knew I held office hours, but I discouraged that. If I needed to see a patient in a month or so, I would give that patient a card reminding them to make an appointment in a month. When that day came, they would phone in the morning, and I would see them in the afternoon.

The most remarkable aspect of a practice such as I had is that it consisted of the lowest possible overhead costs. I could charge less than other physicians charged and still live okay, as long as we drove older used cars, paid for things as we went along and did not borrow money. For fifteen years, we burned only wood to heat the house, which worked fairly well, until the children began having allergy issues relating to the small amounts of smoke in the house. That's when we decided to use an oil furnace with a thermostat—nice invention, those thermostats.

As Mark Hannibal did, I approached my work life with a direct connection to family life and community. Even for Mark to move his business from the Common to Route 17 in Union would have weakened his own link to the community, and he refused to do that. Once the decision is made to limit income in order to express a lifestyle that centers on community, then the parameters of life change. The local culture becomes enriched through diversity, and a man's work becomes his work of art.

Okay, now let's walk down the hill from the Common and talk with Frank Austin.

3

In Sync

Frank Austin and his wife, Josie, live next to the bridge just below the Common, in Sunk Haze, in a house wedged between the river and the road. Though for work Frank now stocks shelves at the Common Market, in my mind, I still see him stamping his boots to keep warm on a winter day as he filled my car's gas tank at Barker's Garage. Never a complaint. But now that Barker's has closed, Frank is at the Common Market, always busy and ready to help if he is needed. He can be seen on the road walking to or from work. When I had an office in my home, Frank would walk the half mile from the garage up the hill for office visits.

Now in his sixties, Frank is quiet and straightforward, his face permanently ruddy from exposure to the elements. His wiry frame serves him well to stock the shelves at the market. Like many Mainers, Frank withholds a smile until the last serious minute.

"Did you work while you were in school here in town?" I asked him.

"I had a paper route, and I raked blueberries and helped with haying and at the canning factory with squash, blueberries and corn. After graduation I worked at the casket factory." Frank seemed nervous; bit his lip.

"What was it like at the casket factory?"

"They were all older. It was a lifetime job, and I worked there some twenty years. I left there to work at the poultry crate factory, but it burned. Then I went back to the casket factory."

The poultry crate factory blaze was before my time. Bobby Heald started the factory, and after it burned, Heald opened a small woodworking shop off Route 17. As one of his projects, he made all the road signs in town, in the form of birdhouses. Now that the town has 9-1-1 emergency services, the roads have been renamed and new street signs have been erected, although the birdhouse signs remain in most places. The road we live on was changed to the Appleton Road; however, in Appleton it is called the Union Road. Depends on which way you're going. After Bobby Heald died, the section of Route 17 through Union was changed and is now called "Heald Highway," but it is the Augusta Road in Washington (the next town to the west) and the Rockland Road in Hope (the next town to the east). Tourists can be seen sitting in their cars pulled over to the side of the road scratching their heads while looking at the map.

"What did you do after you left the casket factory?" I asked.

"During the 1960s I worked part-time for my uncle at his store for a couple of years while I worked at the casket factory. After that, I worked at the garage."

Frank's uncle's store, Gorden's, now the Common Market, burned in 1997, the fire allegedly set by a jealous boyfriend, a migrant worker from an area farm, of a particular female employee. Gary Sukeforth, the subject of the next chapter, bought the property and rebuilt the store, which is today the Common Market where Frank works.

"You're working at Gary's now?"

"For the last two years."

"Do you have any regrets about what you've done for work?"

"Back then, when I went to school, there weren't many opportunities like they have now. Had I to do it now, I would have gone to a trade school, and I could have bettered myself a bit more."

"What do you mean 'bettered'?" I asked.

"If I *had* it to do over again…but I'm not disappointed with myself. You got to remember that there wasn't much to do around here then. For instance, there were only twelve in my graduating class [1953] and all the girls got married, and all the boys went either into the service or to work. None went on to school. We just wanted to get school over with. Later, I realized how good I had it in school."

"Can you envision what you might have been doing if you had gotten more training?"

"I probably wouldn't have worked so long. I like to work, but so *long*…." his voice trailed off.

"What have you enjoyed the most?"

"The garage job, because I was always meeting and talking with people. I meet with people in my job now, too."

When Barker's Garage was operating, men were always standing around jawing, and the Barker brothers threw in their tidbits from beneath a hood or under the lift. Locals left their vehicles at the garage and did not worry about what the mechanics were doing to them. The Barkers ran their business as I ran my medical practice: nothing to sign or fill out and payment was made at the end of the service—face to face.

"How do you see yourself as a worker?"

"I always give a good day's work. I did a good job at the garage, and I never heard anyone complain."

"How did you turn out to be the kind of worker that you are?"

"When I was a kid, things were pretty rough. I wanted my kids to have things that I didn't have. I have to be doing something all the time. I can't sit still."

"Does how you do your work, or the way you approach your work, say anything about your philosophy or religion?"

"I just feel that I should do the best that I can do."

"Why do your best?"

"If the shoe's on the other foot, I would want them to do their best for me."

"That's the Golden Rule," I said. "But where did your attitude come from?"

"I saw my mother work, and she was like that—very dedicated."

"Can you name other workers as dedicated as you are?"

"My son and daughter."

"Do you know others?"

Frank thought for a few moments. "I can't name any," he admitted.

"Are all the good workers working at Wal-Mart?—I don't think so." I laughed at my own joke; Frank did not. "So how did you get to be the way you are?" I asked.

"When I was young I had to go without a lot of things. I just do what has to be done. I don't have to be asked. I just do it. That's the way I want it."

"You sound like the perfect employee."

Frank blushed. "At the garage I was always the last one out of the place. I opened and closed, and I handled the cash. When it was sold, I was the one who locked the door for the last time. I worked there twenty-two years. When I left the garage, I had four or five job offers—people just came to me. As long as I can stay on my feet, I'm working. It's always the way I've been. I see people goofing off, but I just can't do it."

"You've worked for a lot of people. Would you make a good owner of a business?"

"I wouldn't want that responsibility."

"Why not?"

"I don't want the headaches. There's a lot to it. It isn't easy."

"Can you forget about work when you come home?"

"I don't sit around and mill about work."

"Do you ever get fed up with everything? What do you do then?"

"Sometimes I get depressed about things that are going on. I try to let them go. I take a walk. Walking home. Maybe something didn't go good at work—by the time I get home, I more or less forget about it."

Frank expressed something about walking to and from work that I had never thought about before. I see people driving home from work, and I see their stressed looks, sometimes they are talking to themselves. I believe it is easier to reduce stress while exercising.

"Do you have any trouble making decisions?"

"I make my mind up to do something and I just do it. If it's got to be done, I do it."

"When it came to disciplining your own kids, what were you like?"

"I didn't want to be too hard on them, but I made sure they toed the line. We never had any trouble with them."

"What was Josie [his wife] like in disciplining?"

"The same."

"Has there been a person that has really affected you?"

"I'll tell you—it was my mother. She worked two jobs, and there were six kids. When she was sixty-six years old, she got her CNA [Certified Nursing Assistant certificate] and worked at the old Knox Hospital. Maybe that's where I got my work ethic. I took after her. My dad was just the opposite."

"Did your mother place demands on you as children?"

"As soon as we were old enough, we all had to work to keep things going. She was sacrificing, and we took after her."

"How did your brothers and sisters react?"

"Mostly they felt the same. We were a close family—like the Waltons on television. We did all things together."

"Wasn't there fighting and bickering, as in most families?"

"Some, but we got along good."

"How was it that you all got along?"

Frank seemed stuck on that question. He leaned back in his chair. "Gosh—my mother was having it hard—so we all tried to do the best we could. We all respected her: no alcohol, never smoked, hardly ever swore—just a good person, not an enemy in the world."

"How was your father involved?"

"He wasn't working. He was an alcoholic. He saw a lot of action in World War II, and when he came back, he was a different person. He wasn't good to our family. He saw an awful lot. Nowadays they have help for things like that. Not then. He didn't know what he was doing."

In my medical practice, even in the 1970s and 1980s, I had to face the remnants of World War II. Carl, for instance, (not his real name), another WW II veteran, shot and killed himself with his rifle early one morning. Carl called his best friend and then he called me at about 4:00 a.m. to say that we would find his body "out back." An honest man, Carl frequently told me he had blood on his hands from the war—a tank battalion in Italy. He tried to dilute the memories with alcohol. I still have a picture in my mind of Carl's huge white sneakers splayed out from beneath a shroud of black plastic. I sobbed when I got home.

"Sometimes we end up the way we are by being the opposite of a parent," I said. "Do you think that's what happened with you and your father?"

"I didn't hate him for what he did. I didn't hate the man, but I think I was the only kid in the family that felt that way."

"What did he do?"

"Drinking and violent. I heard a lot of what he did in the war, when he and his buddies were drinking and talking. Not good stuff—stuff that really happened. Dead bodies. Killing. I really think it affected his mind. Our home was sort of a gathering place for his drinking friends. He moved out before I left [high] school."

Each town had such an informal meeting and drinking place for WW II vets. Carl, mentioned above, drank with his friends in a neighboring town to Union. Toward the end of it, when his buddies had died, Carl drank alone. The suffering wives of these veterans continued to work and live through it all, usually surviving their husbands by many years.

"Did you ever want to leave town?"

"I was away in the service, but I always said that my home—Union—was the best place. I was born here, and I'll be here when I pass on. I like the country life, the slower pace."

"You have been such an exceptional worker. Have you ever asked for more from your employers?"

"There has never been much to do around here for work. I was glad to be able to work in town and walk to work. I didn't have a lot of the problems that people have at big businesses."

"Do you ever doubt yourself—that you might be different from other men and their approach to work?"

"I'm better off staying here, earning less."

"Do you see yourself as unique, staying this close to home?"

"A lot of people solve that by not working at all," he grinned widely.

"Don't you ever question yourself?"

"No. I don't ever think about it. No," He shook his head.

"You mean you never thought about what you were doing or questioned yourself?"

He thought some more. "Probably I have." He sounded uncertain.

"What did you think about when you did question yourself, maybe when you were middle aged, looking back on your life?"

He thought some more. "I really didn't do that." He gave a sigh of finality. Try as hard as I might, I could find no midlife crisis in this gentleman. That's important to know, I thought.

"Any book affect you?"

"*Come Spring*. I realized that they came up the river, just by my house. I could visualize that. There was a gristmill at Sunk Haze. I found the millstone in my yard. I like history." [*Come Spring* is an historical novel written in 1940 by Ben Ames Williams about the settling of Union after the Revolutionary War.]

"Perhaps one hundred years from now," I said, "people will read this book, and they will see how you felt about your work in Union. That's history."

"I hope to see it myself before I go," he said.

◆   ◆   ◆

I next spoke with Candace, Frank's daughter. Married and in her thirties, Candace lives in a modest house overlooking Seven Tree Pond with her husband and one child. Known for the high quality of her work, she is currently employed, as is her father, at the Common Market. I first met her when she worked in a nursing home. Attractive and sincere, Candace inherited her father's dark curly hair. I asked Candace why her father might have worked so long in Union.

"Dad loves the town," she replied. "For him, Union is *it*. He worked in town, and we only had one vehicle. It was convenient. Mom worked in town, too. I can remember him at the casket factory, and after work, he would clean up at the post office, mow lawns. We didn't have health insurance, so he had to work extra jobs just to pay medical bills. He did most anything he could so we would have a comfortable life."

"Was it comfortable?"

"We had to live with what we had, live within limits—old fashioned values—not around much anymore."

"Did your father talk about these values?"

"Dad was never much of a talker. He's the type that would just go and do something and not talk about it; not want any glory. It's just second nature to him."

"He worked hard," I said. "Did he like it?"

"He never complained. He went to work. Not too many days he didn't work. If he was gone a lot, sometimes, when I was a kid, I would go to work with him and help as best I could. Being in town, you could always see him if you wanted."

"I think I would call the quality that you picked up from your father 'dedication' or 'loyalty,'" I said.

"You work for what you want," she replied. "I don't have high expectations. Grandmother [Frank's mother] used to say that there are so many things and if you want them, it'll just drive you to an early grave. I'll never be in a high paying job, but I'm doing something I feel comfortable with, and I have a sense of accomplishment. I do what has to be done."

"Most people don't approach their work as you do," I said.

"I don't really know," she replied shaking her head. "I stay in my own world."

"Your father has essentially said the same things to me," I said. Candace smiled. "What was he like when you were younger? Did he make you and your brother toe the line?"

"Both my mother and he made sure that we both were on the right path. My brother and I just didn't want to get into trouble. We understood that whatever we did wrong would be with us the rest of our lives; and if we did the right thing, we would have nothing to worry about."

"Is that something that was passed through your family, or is it a moral issue coming from religion?"

"It's a family value, but we did go to church on Sundays."

"Don't you ever get fed up with things, wanting stuff you don't have, frustrated with your life in general?"

"That's human nature," she replied with ease. "When I feel like that, I have to talk things through—with my husband—get the issues out, especially about raising the family."

"That's much different than with your father."

"True. He would go outside rather than have a scene in front of us."

"How did it come about that you use communication in a different manner?"

"Mostly trial and error. Before we got married, we had counseling with the minister. That got the process started. But you've got to remember that I didn't go through the same things that my father did."

"You must have felt that you wanted something different."

"I don't like leaving things up in the air. I like to solve things, follow through to the end."

"Were you more like your grandmother in terms of your communication skills, or more like your dad in that respect?"

"More like my dad, but Grandmother was in an abusive marriage. She stayed with it through thick and thin, worked three jobs just to keep the family together. She was quite old when she finally divorced. That's maybe why Dad always wanted to keep things smooth, not make waves. He realized that his father was an alcoholic, but Dad would never drink more than one drink. He went through a lot. He never complained."

What Candace was saying rang a bell in my head, not just because she described her father as both unwavering and non-complaining as she did her grandmother, but also because I had seen in my medical practice so many similar situations in that World War II generation. Here was a state of affairs with her grandmother that today we would readily label as abusive, and experts would say that her grandmother was enabling her grandfather, that she should set limits and, if necessary, kick him out of the house. However, I know that those women from that day and age would not listen to such a thing, and that they would continue to slog forward loyally as best they could, just to get through. Loyalty or enabling—make your choice.

To my way of seeing it, Frank took a large step by holding close the loyalty he learned from his mother, and he and his wife, Josie, provided the important peaceful atmosphere that allowed his children to develop their own selves. I saw the resolution of a problem through three generations. Candace and her brother were the synthesis of the two previous generations.

"I have one more question that's bothering me: Have you ever traveled much?"

"Not really. As a family, we went to Florida for a short time. We saved our money to do it. It's not a priority in trying to raise a family. Other things are more important."

"How much should kids be exposed to?"

"Kids with each generation are more aware of things. You can't keep them sheltered from the real world, but I wonder if you can go too far, their seeing so many things quicker than they really need to."

I came away from these two interviews with Frank and Candace feeling positive about small town life, and life in general. Sometimes things work out for the best. Now I needed to talk with Josie—Frank's wife and Candace's mother.

◆　　　◆　　　◆

I have an image of Josie at school, where she works with confidence in the school kitchen, ladling out food with a friendly comment as the children pass by holding their trays. In work, she wears an apron and a baseball cap. At home, I had to look twice to recognize Josie in a dress and her hair nicely curled. Sturdy built and handsome like her daughter, Josie is unafraid to look at you.

"How did you meet Frank?" I asked.

"Through the sister-in-law of his sister. We both worked at Sylvania."

Sylvania ran a light bulb filament plant in Waldoboro, a manufacturing plant being a rare thing along the Maine coast—with the exception of boatbuilding. The plant provided a semblance of independence for many a woman throughout the years, including my mother-in-law. As a group, the Sylvania women always knew what was going on in the surrounding communities.

"You didn't go to school with Frank?"

"No, I was from Friendship [along the coast]. I met him later. We went together for six months and got married. I moved to Union, but I continued to work at Sylvania for five more years. Then Candace came along. I got done at Sylvania and stayed at home during the days, but did seasonal work at the canning factories, mostly at night. Then Darren was born. Frank stayed with them at night when I worked."

"Frank was working in town at that time. Did he ever mention anything about working elsewhere or getting some training?"

"I always told him that he could do anything." she replied sharply, but her eyes were friendly.

"What did he say?"

"He's not one to talk."

"So how would you know that he was even thinking about those things?"

"I don't. But I knew that he would get discouraged sometimes when he was being taken advantage of."

"You mean that he lacked the confidence to say anything?"

"He likes this town. He grew up here, and he's just content to live and work in his hometown. He's not scared of work, never has been."

"Do you think his desire to live and work in Union has made for a good life?"

"He seems contented. His father was a fine carpenter, but he didn't work much, because he drank."

"Can Frank do carpentry?"

"Oh, he can do anything if he gets up the confidence to do it. He would say that he couldn't do something, and I'd say that he *could* do it. He needs somebody to urge him."

"Did you know his mother very well?"

"His mother was a mother to *me*, even more than my own. She was a wonderful woman. Hard worker. Wicked abused. Never complained. We stuck with her, right up until she died in the nursing home."

"So Frank took after his mother rather than his father."

"If 'twas the other way around, I would have planted him in the back yard long ago. The first day I met his father, he was drunk."

"Frank was?"

"No, I've never seen Frank drunk. Maybe one drink now and then, but never before driving."

"When I talk to Frank, he sounds like the perfect employee, and I know him to be that good from my own experience."

"They took advantage of him."

"Did he fret about that?"

"Not really, but at times he would get upset. Less now that he's older."

"The bottom line, though, your kids seemed to have turned out well," I said.

"I always told my kids—no matter what you do I'll always love you, but I may not always like what you do."

"Did you both work at discipline?"

"He [Frank] might holler at them, but I felt that I was the one who set the limits. Sometimes I would get kinda disgusted—but what's the use? I figured it might be from his childhood—sad thing. He never had much. He told me he had only one happy Christmas—there was a dollar for him on the Christmas tree, but by the end of the day even that was gone for beer [for his father]."

"Was there open communication in your home?"

"If an issue came up, he didn't want any part of it. He'd pass it off."

"Candace is a good communicator. How did that come about?"

"I think that came from Frank's mother. If everybody could be only one-eighth of how she was, it would be a good world."

Again, I was reminded of how Frank's mother's goodness extended through the generations.

"How long have you worked at the school?"

"Thirty-two years in April. The main thing was to either be at home for the kids, or be with them at work. I wanted to be with my kids."

"You're a strong woman."

"I never *was*. I was made independent out of necessity. When I was young and we had people over, I would go into the bedroom. I just couldn't stand groups of people. Shy, I guess. But now I love people."

"How did you carry out that transformation?"

"I don't know. I just did it. Someone had to be strong."

"Frank, with all his ability, I never saw him in a job that required a great amount of decision making. Maybe he didn't want to do anything wrong? A lot of people are like that, but I don't want to put words in your mouth."

"Yes," she replied, nodding her head, "I think that's true."

"There's something we're missing here," I said, "and I'm not sure I can put it into words. Frank comes out of an abusive home life with a wonderful mother who nowadays would be termed an enabler, maybe mistakenly."

"She wasn't about to move out. That was her home. She owned it."

"Frank comes out of that home life without much confidence, for whatever reason."

"And he became a workaholic, not an alcoholic," she replied. "He's always better off doing something. Got to be doing something—can't seem to relax."

"Yet" I said, "I can't see Candace becoming the person she is today without her having the advantage of a peaceful home life in which she was able, freely, to find her own way."

"Well, he didn't want to rattle the cage—anyone's."

"All I'm trying to say is that *if* Frank was more ambitious and more forceful in his ways, then your whole life would have taken on a much different character, and some of that would not have been positive, and there would have been more conflict and less peace. Maybe his fear was legitimate, and if he overcame it, it would have destroyed the life he wanted in this town: performing a low-stress job, walking to work, not having to supervise or be responsible for others...ability, without ambition," I half muttered to myself.

"Then people will take advantage," she quickly threw in.

"But, if he spoke up, he risked his job. All the employers here are small, and their margins are just that—small."

"That's what *he* always said. But there's no harm in speaking up within reason. Some of them are decent enough to understand."

"He lines up on the side of the meek," I said. "And his life would be so different if he wasn't that way. The bottom line is whether all the sacrifices are worth it."

"Our kids turned out good—people tell me that—but lots of times the clothes they wore were handed down four times. I had to patch the pockets, fix the buttonholes. When they got older, they bought their own sneakers. Kids today, they have too much—'course I'm from an older generation."

"It's a paradox," I said. "All the positive things that have gone along in your and Frank's life in this town are so different from what television and the other media, and even the schools, are aiming at."

"I'm content right here," she replied. "I love the kids. I love the people. I can say that I really like my job. A lot of people can't say that."

◆   ◆   ◆

Though not overtly religious, Frank and Josie base their lives on fundamentals: honesty, hard work, concern for the welfare of others. These are the fundamentals of all religions. If some people see Frank as lacking self-confidence, the core of that uncertainty may very well come from a misfit with what he is and what our broader culture deems a successful man must be. That can cause angst in any man, admitted or not.

We will now return to the Common, because it will be instructive to talk with Gary Sukeforth, the man who employs Frank.

4

One on One

Gary Sukeforth, owner of the Common Market and Frank Austin's employer, sat in my small office in a straight chair. He would have preferred propping his feet on something, as I was doing while interviewing him, but there was no place to put his feet except the floor, so he crossed and uncrossed them uncomfortably, always shifting in his chair. He wore his usual baggy khakis, a checkered long-sleeved shirt and his baseball hat with rounded brim—his dark hair curling up on the sides beneath the hat. He has a boyish face, rather full, but accented by a look of wonder, detectable only when he doesn't have a couple day's growth of dark beard. I was surprised to learn that he is only forty-two years old.

I did the interview in two parts, and the very last section took place in Gary's office above his store. Of piles of papers and clutter, Gary was the champion, besting even me.

"You're in the grocery business," I said. "Tell me how that came about."

He took a deep breath and exhaled. "I was the youngest of nine kids, and I was raised in Appleton [north of Union] as a fundamentalist Baptist of the likes of Jerry Falwell. My mother taught Sunday school.

"When I was young," he continued, "I sort of thought that I would be a minister, but as I got older, I just couldn't swallow that whole ball of wax. I could have done better in high school. I think I have ADD [attention deficit disorder] and I'm disorganized, but I graduated, and I was admitted to Georgetown University. I wanted to go into economics, but I got a deferred enrollment and traveled. I went west and looked at other schools, but when I returned, I still had time until school started; so I got a job at Crowe Rope in Warren [south of Union]. A while later, I ended up enrolling at UMO [University of Maine in Orono] and majored in agricultural economics. I did well.

"After I graduated I didn't know what I wanted to do, but I went to graduate school for two years at Penn. State in agricultural economics. After graduation, I got a job in the commodities exchange in Chicago. I worked on the floor, first as a runner, later taking orders on the phone. It was hectic and as much as I liked it—and I was good at it—philosophically I couldn't accept it."

"Did it bother you to go to Chicago and begin a new job?"

"No. I'm not easily overwhelmed, or under-whelmed, for that matter. I just don't get emotional about things."

"Why could you not philosophically accept the commodities market?"

"It was too money-driven, and there was too much manipulative behavior. Even when I was in graduate school, I knew my heart wasn't in it. For instance, I have no interest in the stock market."

"Why not the stock market?"

"I have a hard time investing in a company if I don't know how they treat their employees, or how they relate to their community. Most people only invest in the market to make money. I know there's green funds, but I feel that if a company does well, it's because of the workers. Every company ultimately belongs to the workers. For myself, I'd rather make money by being more productive."

"If you weren't interested in making money in Chicago, what were you interested in?"

"I was becoming more interested in psychology and religion. I had been thinking about moving back to Maine and buying some land from my parents, but around that time my father died, and I did move back. My mother was alone—none of my other brothers and sisters lived at home—and she rattled around in that big old house."

"Did you seek out your religious or psychological interests while you were still in Chicago?"

"I lived near a Unitarian Universalist (UU) church, and I happened to read in the newspaper about a new minister there. The article interested me. The guy was an atheist and gay, and it was this sort of open-mindedness that I was looking for in a church, even though I wasn't either one of those things. At the first service I attended, they had a rock and roll band. Some members of that particular church also had regular beer and poker society meetings—something that did interest me."

"You come from a fundamentalist background, yet you have this open-minded acceptance of other people. How did that come about?"

"I remember in high school, it was the energy crisis and the time of Jimmy Carter, and I became sort of a hippie-type, interested in the *Mother Earth News*. I was certainly more 'granola' than my upbringing. Through it all, though, I remained rational and analytical. I was exposed to only one religion, but I looked at all religions as paths. I suppose if I had kids, I would probably take them to a

UU church; but I'm still glad I had the upbringing that I did, even though I can't accept all of it. Does that make sense?"

"It does to me," I replied, "if you consider that all religions contain the same truths, but you strike me as a person who would refuse to hook into any conceptual framework for fear of having to cast aside, from time to time, your rational sense."

He considered for a few moments. "Yes, I think that's true."

"What did you do after you returned to Maine?"

"When I got home in Maine, I took a job with the State doing statistical research, and I became involved in town government. A short time later, I ran for selectman in Appleton and won. As a selectman, I found myself frustrated, because even though we always had public meetings, people kept complaining that they never knew what was going on. So I started the *Appleton Monthly*, a newsletter to inform the people of the goings-on of the town.

"I soon learned that other selectmen in other towns had the same problem, and rather than try to do a bunch of different newsletters, *Good Neighbors* was born and replaced the *Appleton Monthly*. [*Good Neighbors* became a monthly newspaper with articles and advertising in a five town rural area.]

"Wait a minute," I said. "You jumped from a newsletter to a newspaper. That's a big jump."

Gary laughed, I think at himself. "I bought a light-table," he said, "a hand waxer and some of the tools you need for cutting and pasting, and I fixed up a little room in my house for it. I had read a book about how to produce your own small newspaper."

Then I laughed. "Weren't you a bit nervous about doing this for the first time?"

"I hired Lynn Allen to help me. She had worked for the *Camden Herald*. It was a few days before press time, the very first paper, and she came over to help. I sort of pushed all the stuff in front of her. She asked me if I had ever done anything like that before, and of course, I hadn't. I thought we would figure it out. And we did, but she was startled that I would become the owner and editor of a newspaper without having any experience. I guess I could have come out looking like a fool."

"When did you move your operation to Union?"

"In 1991 I quit my job with the State, and I knew I couldn't make a living with *Good Neighbors*, so I took space on the Union Common and started the Cricket [an office supply, gift and novelty store on the Common]. It gave me a job and a storefront for *Good Neighbors*. I saw a need for a store like the Cricket, just as I had seen the need for the general store up in Burkettville [bordering Union]. I had gotten some family members together to do that—now it's the only store there.

"After Gorden's store burned I really wasn't involved in what they were going to do. I helped with some fund-raising and publicity, but I discovered that some-one was proposing a strip mall off the Common. I was getting calls about what to do, and I said that I would research it. The Masons [The Masons owned the building and had their meetings on the second floor] eventually decided that they didn't want to relocate on the Common, and they offered to sell me the land for $1 if I would build and run a market. After easements, approvals and more fund-ing sources, we opened February 2000—for better or worse."

"You live at the store now?"

"On the second level. It's a lot of hours—I want to do a good job—but maybe it's more correct that I don't want to do a bad job. I'm indifferent to it, not ambivalent. It's a job that needs doing. I stopped publishing the newspaper, not that I didn't like it, but I just couldn't stand the stress of getting it out each month. Writing doesn't come natural to me, and I don't miss the grunt work. I still own the Cricket. That's my baby, and I don't want to sell. It's not that I want to take on more all the time, but I see things that I want to do—things that I think need to be done. You could call them goals."

"When you were working behind the counter at the Cricket, I can remember going in there and seeing all sorts of women hanging around. You're a bache-lor...." Gary started to laugh. "Do you think there was any connection?"

Still laughing, he replied, "Honestly, that went over my head. I never thought about it, but you need to remember that it's women who buy the jewelry, the cards, candles."

"Sure," I said. "What's it like living upstairs in your store now. When do you sleep?"

"I'm usually done by 11 p.m. Actually, I'm never done. My day starts at 3:30 in the morning. They make the deliveries at 3:45. I like living in town, but I still look forward to when I can return to the farm."

"You mentioned goals."

"I own the family farm—forty-five acres and the house—and I want to make it a productive, financially self-sustaining and ecologically sound unit—not a gentleman's farm, but to show that a productive farm can be done with forty-five acres. I have a retail outlet. That's a big thing. Most farmers don't own a grocery store.

"I also want to start a UU church or fellowship in Union. I think there are a lot of potential UU's out there, and I am confident it will come to fruition.

"I want to organize a community band. There's a lot of folks of all ages out there that can play musical instruments. We have the bandstand on the Common already. I have approached someone about being a director. I'm tone deaf myself."

"Do you want to do these projects yourself, or do you mind if someone else does them?"

"I like doing things, but I would be satisfied if someone else did them—*properly*."

"To me, you sound very practical."

"Money doesn't mean much to me. I grew up in a family that was pretty poor. My father worked at the button factory in Waldoboro, then after his heart attack, he sold vegetables at home. My mother did housework for rich people in Camden. I'm just not into things. I see needs, but I'm indifferent to money. Some call me cheap, but I'm frugal. I don't like waste."

"Do you carry over much of your early religious training into your life now?"

"A lot of people brought up as fundamentalists hold it against their parents. I see that in UU all the time. I knew fairly early that it wasn't for me, but I don't resent it. Those religious values are good values, and I'm glad I had them ingrained in me. I just had to drop all that dogma."

"You remind me of Benjamin Franklin," I said.

"Yes, I remember reading about his religious beliefs, and he said that he was a deist, that he thought he was blessed, but he thought that all the dogma about the Trinity got blown out of proportion, even though he believed that the morals coming from Jesus were very good."

"How do you make your major decisions?"

"I don't analyze myself much, but I do get sort of a gut feeling about things—whether they will work or not. I do want to make the world a better place to live in, but you know, you must start with yourself. Very few people can change the world to any degree. You have to do just your small part, but the first step is to start with yourself."

"And it has to be economically feasible," I said.

"Economics is important. I'm mortgaged to the hilt, but whatever I do has to pay its own way. Some businesses are just in the wrong place, but there's a matter of fairness. I wouldn't want to subsidize my farm with other income, because it would be unfair to other farmers in the area that have to make do on what they have."

"You don't believe in survival of the fittest?"

"The world is too complex for that," he replied. "There are so many companies that are subsidized in many different ways—tax subsidies—you name it. Survival of the fittest doesn't apply any more."

"Then fairness is important to you," I stated.

"I could probably have convinced the town to give me a property tax incentive to build the grocery store. I believe in government and private companies working together, but if they gave me a tax break, then they would have to raise that much more from everyone else in the town, even from some guy that didn't want to use my store. It's not right."

"Do you have heroes?"

"I don't believe in heroes. I don't believe that a person should look up. Everyone has a light inside. They have to look inside, not anywhere else. If they look for it, it will guide them."

"Do you think there is chaos in this universe, or is it ordered?"

"If there is chaos, it's caused by the wills of all the individuals. Outcome is the result of individual actions. Self exists, and it is made better by prayer and meditation where we can work on ourselves."

"That puts all the responsibility onto you—and everybody else," I replied.

"I have the ability and capabilities to take responsibility," he said. "The biggest responsibility of all is being a parent. By not being a parent or a husband though, I can take on *additional* responsibilities."

"Do you feel burdened?"

"I've always said that if I ever won the Megabucks, I would move to a warm climate—maybe Florida—and I would live in a cardboard box in a ditch somewhere and hire two people: one to keep the snakes away, and the other to get my beer. That idea is sort of at the other end of the spectrum from where I am with responsibility. Sometimes I wish I didn't have all that on my back."

"I like the cardboard box," I said. "You appear not to be competitive with yourself, or with others."

"That's right. I don't feel driven."

"When a person takes on responsibility to fill a need," I said, "and that person seeks to fill that need intelligently and without an eye for personal gain, the person is usually doing it for a perceived higher purpose. What would be your higher purpose?"

"I don't consider that. Why consider that?" he shrugged. "These values were ingrained in me at an early age. I feel like it's the right thing for me. I just do it."

"Without thought?"

"I guess you could say that I am in a constant state of prayer—I'm always aware, aware of—a state of oneness. It's sort of a different plane from the one on which most people live, I think."

"Any books that you found helpful?"

"E.F. Schumacher's *Small is Beautiful* and his later book, *Guide to the Perplexed*. I was able to relate to Peck's *The Road Less Traveled*. He talked about aloneness versus loneliness. Aloneness is not the same as being lonely—I know what it is."

"Do you feel alone?"

"Sometimes it seems as if I'm antisocial, but I'm tired, and I'm busy. Part of me *is* alone."

"You've been elected to the state legislature. How do you meld your politics with your philosophy?"

"I ran as an independent, but only because I didn't feel comfortable in any party. I'm not into hoopla. But now that I've a session behind me, and I look at my voting record, it looks more conservative than anything—I never would have guessed that before."

"How did that come about?"

"It has to do with core society values, and you have to get back to some sense of individual responsibility when you try to solve things for people. People still have to step up to the plate. In legislation, there may be more than one issue—fairness, economics, public health—and I don't look on it as black and white, because it isn't black or white. I tend in the direction of encouraging people to be more responsible. Yet not everyone is dealt the same hand, and some need help through no fault of their own.

"But in Augusta, you have to vote, and then it's black or white, yes or no, no matter how complex the issue. It's easier if you're true blue Democrat or Republican, because then you just vote with the party. If I can see both sides 60/40, then with that, I tend to be more conservative. When in doubt, I feel it's best not to be intrusive, and the less government the better. One thing's for sure: If you give a tax break to anyone, someone else is going to have to pay.

"I accept that people can look at problems differently, and most of my values seem to be in the minority, not that others are definitely wrong and I am right, or that they should not be allowed to do what they are doing." He gave a long sigh. "Dirigo Health, for instance [Maine's determination to have a State-run single-payer health care system]. God knows we're in a crisis and something has to be done, but I can't make that leap—especially for businesses. I simply can't accept one plan that is supposed to fit all. Each person's situation is different in life."

"I never understood how businesses ever got involved with providing health insurance in the first place." I said.

"I didn't know that, either, until recently," he replied. "It apparently got started during World War II, when there was both a wage freeze and also a shortage of labor. To compete in the labor market, businesses resorted to offering health insurance."

"You talk much about individual responsibility," I said. "Does that have relation to the 'oneness' that you describe in your continuous state of prayer? Does each person have a spark of divine individuality, and in that way, we all form part of one system?"

"No, that's not what I mean." He stopped to think for a moment. "Using Dirigo Health as an example, by responsibility I mean the State has the responsibility to make a medium for a fair market for this insurance. And businesses, because they no longer have to pay health insurance premiums, the money they save should go back to the employees. And the employees, they must assume more responsibility for good health—with built-in incentives. It's just too easy for everyone involved not to pay attention to what they are doing just because someone else, including the government, is paying for it."

"So everyone has responsibility around certain core values in our society?"

"In a way, but it seems that we are giving up individual responsibilities in small incremental steps, and if we keep going, we will take a step too far, even though there's lots of people out there—especially kids—that are in situations from no fault of their own, and they need a safety net."

"A thin edge you walk upon," I said.

He nodded, "Yes, it's thin."

"I still don't understand your oneness."

"I look at things using reason. All my business decisions are rational, but even with that, there's always a leap of faith in any endeavor. In religion, it's the same. If I look at life reasonably, then I have to admit that I am an agnostic. A lot of fundamentalists say they have conversations with God, and that they know God, but there's still no proof of that. *Spiritually*, I believe in God."

"You are one with God?"

"You could say that my oneness is my individual connection to a higher power. In this world today, there are many people without a religious compass in everyday life, but I had that as a child. I can't imagine not growing up in a house without any religious or spiritual guidance. This oneness is my life, and I don't know what I could use if I didn't have it." He relaxed in his chair.

"So, Gary, are you going to run for the legislature again?"

"That's the big question," he replied, sitting up again. "At least it's the big question for the Democrats and the Republicans, because I'm an independent, and I don't have to declare until the last minute—not having to go through a primary. The longer I can wait on a decision the more information I have, and the better the decision will be. That's what I think."

I always thought that waiting until the last minute was a particularly Maine trait, mostly brought on by the weather. I remember in southern California, a person could always plan ahead, because the weather would be dependably good. That gives people a sense of omnipotence that I call the "California neurosis." In Maine, the weather cuts you down to size. No choice. You must wait and see.

"I think, Gary, you are one of the few truly compassionate conservatives."

"Yes," he said, a bit sadly. "I seem to reach a conservative end, but the path I take to get there is my own."

"You may be onto something, my friend."

◆   ◆   ◆

Gary keeps company with many creative people who know that they stand solitary with the expression of their ideas. Gary anchors himself with his belief in God, and with that anchor, he experiences the world through what he calls a "constant state of prayer." He believes in an inner light that he uses for guidance. Some people want to lead their lives in constant relationship with their souls.

Let's return now to Frank Austin's house and resume our short walk back to the Common.

5

Through the Wringer

We can begin to feel the moist air of the St. George River as we walk down the hill from Frank Austin's home to the pocket-sized settlement of Sunk Haze where we cross a bridge. The small river roils over its banks during the spring, but lazes during the summer. Climbing the short steep hill to the Common, we see Dwinal Tripp's house on the right, built close to the road just below the Cricket. The old stake-bodied truck Dwinal uses to collect the trash rests in front. I always know if Dwinal has removed the trash from our barn, because I can see a drip of oil on the driveway where the truck idled, and a few drips trailing up the drive-way. Some things never seem to change, and I guess Dwiny keeps adding oil [though since this writing, the drips have stopped].

Dwiny, a burly middle-aged fellow with an easy smile and a propensity to choose words carefully, took over the trash route when Bill Hastings died. Our kids called Bill, "Wild Bill." Bill had worked at the casket factory for years, and he enjoyed his beer and picking up the trash on Fridays. Unfortunately, he suffered a stroke several years ago and died. Dwiny took over the route with a little uncertainty at first.

Dwiny and I were sitting in my office when I asked him what he would call the work he does.

"Picking up household trash," he replied. "They've got some fifty-cent words for it—I can't even think of them right now—'engineering' something. You probably know what I'm talking about."

"How long have you been doing this?"

"I worked for Bill for fourteen years, but after Bill died, I've only done this since."

"You own the business now?"

"Girlfriend and I."

"What's the most difficult part of what you do?"

"Recycling. It's not hard, but it's time-consuming."

"What do you think of your job?"

"I love it," he replied, without hesitation.

"Why?"

"In the long run, I'm saving the taxpayers money."

"Do you have a lot to think about with this business?"

"Girlfriend has quite a lot of paperwork—keeping track."

"Do you feel you are providing a real service?"

"I believe it."

"What's behind that service?"

"I'm doing—maybe a favor for the people. I get to talk to some of the people, and I enjoy it."

"Are the people fair?"

"They really are. If I'm usually there at 8:30, then at 8:25 I'm too early, and at 8:35, I'm too late. I don't punch a time card, I tell 'em—if they're talking to me—it involves the time for the next guy. They don't realize it until I bring it up."

"Are they ugly?"

"They understand. Just like everybody—they think you're there at the exact same time every day."

"Does your work bother you in any way after you get home, at the end of the day?"

"It's totally out of mind."

"How about with Dale [Dwiny's girlfriend]?"

"She doesn't mind the paperwork. Someone might call at night and ask about taking a mattress or some such, and she tells them what it would cost. She knows that some of those people are on fixed income, so she might fret about that and maybe not charge what it ends up costing us. She's a CNA at the hospital. She's used to people and can put a smile on her face and still be upset with this business."

"Don't you ever get fed up with this business?"

"No. I enjoy it."

"Do you take time off?"

"I don't need the time, so I don't take the time. If I wanted to do something, then I would do it. I'm that type."

"Before you picked up trash, what did you do?"

"I worked as a weaver at Knox Woolen [in Camden]. I also cut firewood before I went to work in the mornings."

"What was it like working for the woolen mill?"

"You always knew that if you could punch a time card that you had work. Even if you had a broken arm or leg, you could work. Everyone was like a family. I would've been working there still if they hadn't closed, believe me."

A competitor bought out the mill and later closed it. The mill sat vacant for many years until MBNA, the world's largest independent credit card issuer, bought it and completely rebuilt the structure. MBNA now has their telemarketing division there. Dominating the town as it does, MBNA appears to continue in the mill tradition in Camden, and now in Belfast and Rockland—three towns in a line along the coast of Maine. Time will tell if it will disappear mill fashion sometime down the road. (In fact, subsequent to this interview, MBNA moved out of Camden, and then Rockland.)

"If you have an idea about something, maybe to change something, how do you handle it?"

"I procrastinate. If I do get an idea, I'll mention it to someone, and maybe they'll try it first."

"What if it's something that you might need to do?"

"I'll talk to my girlfriend, or either of my sisters, or my brother, because I figure they can tell me whether I should do it or not."

"How would you determine whose advice to take?"

"I try to think of who would give me the most honest opinion, but they all know that it'll be my final decision."

"When you ask for advice, will the person that advises you take credit for your decision if you follow the advice?"

"They forget about it. With my personality, they know that I really wanted to know, or else I wouldn't ask."

"If you don't take their advice, and the project turns sour, do they come back on you and say that you should have done...something else?"

"They might, jokingly. But to me, it's a closed door. Once I make a decision, that's it. I don't second-guess. Right or wrong, we move on."

"Was buying the business a difficult decision?"

"I talked it over with my girlfriend, and it's her and I. She does the financial and the physical part, along with me, and I bought the truck. Bill had a good many friends, and I didn't know if they would want me. Also, there are a lot of elderly ones that will pass on."

"How are your relations with the people at the [Union] transfer station?"

"It's smooth. After you learn their ways all you have to do is abide by them. The people at the dump are really wonderful. They'll even come out and help if they're not busy."

"You are doing a service by recycling, and also disposing of unwanted items. Otherwise, people would have to do it themselves. You are receiving some type of fulfillment from this job. Tell me about that."

"It gives me a great feeling to be able to do it. Sometimes I put the mail in the mailbox for them, or I might remove an air conditioner out of a window. They really like the help. Sometimes they make me cookies."

"So it's much more than just trash removal."

"Yes, it really is. They make you feel wanted—they really do."

"Have you always had your current attitude?"

"I enjoy meeting people. Ever since I was a kid, I had a good outlook on life. I always said that it's just as easy to smile. People pick up on that very quickly."

"Then by being friendly, people are more likely to ask for help. Is that it?"

"Yes, yes."

"Is it necessary for you to think about religious or philosophical things to be how you are?"

"More so since I lost my wife—in '95."

"Death makes you start to think about those things?"

"Somebody that close to you—that young—it's time to do some serious thinking."

"Did that experience change you?"

"It made me stronger as a person. Everything bad in life, something good also happens down the road."

"What do you mean by 'stronger'?"

"Back before she got sick, she handled all, you know, the children, the domestic stuff—not all, but mostly. After she got sick and died, I had to learn to cook. I always figured house chores were not a big deal until I done 'em myself."

"What is the chore situation with Dale and you now?"

"We split the chores. I do the cooking and laundry."

"So, before your wife died, you figured that the housework was the woman's job?"

He smiled. "I did think that was the way of it."

"Your daughter is now living with you. How about your son in Thomaston, does he help at his home?"

"He's pretty much like I used to be, except he helps more with the kids."

"It sounds like you show kindness in your work. Is your work all the fulfillment that you need along those lines?"

"Yes, it is."

"If you had to do it all over again, would you be doing what you are now?"

"Under the same circumstances, yes."

"What is an ideal job to you?"

"I believe this is it. I really do."

"Not many people can make that statement," I said.

"I've been fortunate to do three jobs I really enjoyed [woolen mill, firewood and trash removal]. A lot of people work, and they don't enjoy what they're doing. I've never had a stressful job. I couldn't do something I didn't enjoy."

"There are many people who would say that they could never do what you do, that they would not be happy doing it. Yet you seem to love it. Can you give any advice to them about being happy in work?"

"The way I see things, the people who are unhappy are the ones that let money do the talking. I understand that point of view, but I'd rather have something that paid less and be happy with it. I don't need a new car or a new home. I see how these other people live, and it scares me. I've been fortunate that way."

"Did you ever think about having more training, or perhaps getting into a trade?"

"I don't need a trade, and if I had to sit behind a desk, I'd be stressed right out."

"Don't you feel alone, as you're the only one around that does what you do and the way you do it?"

"Oh, there's others that does it, but they don't last long."

I laughed. "There's an old Chinese saying, 'It's easy to open a store, but awful hard to keep it open.' You said a bit ago that it scares you what other people do for money."

"Yes, it does scare me. For instance, I could buy a compactor for my truck, and it would cost me $80,000. Then it *would be* stressful, and I would have to compete."

"There's something to say for low technology," I said. "All my wife has ever had in the office is a Rolodex: it's never off-line, and it never breaks down."

Dwiny was nodding.

◆   ◆   ◆

I asked Dwiny's girlfriend, Dale, for an interview. Dale and Dwiny have lived together for seven years. We sat in our kids' study room, because Butler, Maxcy & Heath was installing a new gas fireplace in our living room. No trees to cut, no wood to split and carry, no soot, no chimney fires—wow, what a cop out.

Dale is a large woman who moves about easily. She has longish blonde hair and a way of holding up her head when she answers a question that makes you feel as though she only tells the truth.

"You were living with Dwiny when he took over the trash business. How did you get involved?"

"It had only been a week or two, and Tripper—I call him Tripper—was having a hard time finding anyone to depend on for help. I said I would help him for awhile, and..." She gestured as if to say "here I am."

"Is working together different from living together?"

"He had his ways, and it's hard for him to change—set in his ways, he is—but after a while he would listen to me."

"After four years of your working with him, is it more 50/50?"

"Yes. It's looked upon as a man's job, but I do the driving sometimes—do what he does."

"How about at home?"

"He does the major cooking, the laundry. We share."

"After his wife died, he says that he changed."

"I think it was difficult for him, as he always had women taking care of him. It was, mostly still is, a man's world. I was born and brought up here."

"You work at the hospital as a CNA. Is that something you need to do to maintain your lifestyle?"

"I like keeping my independence. I've always held down two or three jobs, and now it's more than just the money."

"Is Dwiny a bit old fashioned?"

"*Is* he," she laughed. "He grew up without much. Take that old wringer washer of his. Somebody ought to tell him what century this is."

"You mean he uses a wringer washer?"

"Sure he does, and he loves it. He'd cry a bucket if it was gone. I threaten him that I'm going to burn it sometime. He was put back a bit when the Laundromat burned."

"He used the Laundromat?"

"For drying, sometimes." I do recall seeing clothes hanging out behind Dwiny's house, even in iffy weather.

My wife's father was so old fashioned that he balked at hot running water—preferred an outside well—and he refused any heat but wood heat, used horses in his woodcutting business, and certainly no indoor plumbing was allowed. My wife's mother finally put her foot down and went to work at the Sylvania plant in Waldoboro, and she soon lifted the household into the twentieth century.

"Is it stressful having two jobs, one in town and one in Rockland?" I asked.

"I'd be happy just to do garbaging, but that's not full-time. It's not so stressful as dealing with life and death matters with patients, and you get outside, ride around."

"Dwiny says that he procrastinates before he makes a decision."

"He's awful. I've never met anyone like he is—and I never figured out why he's like that."

"Can you give me an example?"

"Oh, he saw a riding lawnmower on sale at Sears, and the doctor told him he shouldn't push a mower, but he never went back, and when he did, he had to pay more. He kept saying that he should have bought it before."

"Maybe he puts off decisions until he's forced into it?"

"I think that's right," she said. "After Bill died, he hemmed and hawed. I told him to just do it—people will still want you. Sometimes, with men, you have to kick them in the butt."

"Is it the fear of failure?"

"I have to deal with men in the hospital, and most of them are really scared, but they won't admit it. For instance, if they've had a knee done, and you want them to put their foot on the floor, they'll really hesitate; but a woman will jump down and just do it."

"Why is that?"

"Men are just brought up that way. When Tripper had his bypass, and later the defibrillator and pacemaker, he pretended that it didn't bother him."

"Going through that would bother me," I said. I hadn't known about his surgery.

"He never dwells on it. He believes that when you're gonna die, you'll just die. But in the hospital, he was scared. I know about those things. My ex-husband had a bypass. What with the tubing and all, I knew what the feelings would be. Men, a lot of times, they're just plain scared, and they don't know how to say it. They're scared of emotions—and they don't like being alone."

"The women of Maine strike me as being a strong lot," I said.

"Many women I know, they raise their children alone. They're generationally strong."

"Maybe the men of Maine don't have much exposure to a father figure when they're very young."

"Yeah. Most of them rarely see their fathers, except on Sunday. I tell the younger women that I work with, when they ask me about dating, that the first thing you look for is the guy's relationship with his mother and father. If he doesn't get along with his mother, then he'll have trouble with other women, and if he hates his father, then there's lots of problems."

I know from my exposure to families in Union, fathers who take care of their children all along are more in touch with their emotions and generally more real. That's what happens when you take care of children. Women know that.

"What was your upbringing like?"

"I lived in Camden. My father committed suicide when I was eight. My mother was left with the five of us, with the youngest less than a year old."

"Did you have to work a lot, or were you allowed to be a kid?"

"I could be a kid. We had a big family around, and they helped. My older brother was married, and he helped. My mother remarried, a good man, a great stepfather."

"You're bright, and you could do just about anything you set your mind to. Did you ever think about getting more training?"

"School was never a big thing to me—I didn't graduate from high school—later I got a GED. Now I give out the medicines as a med-tech. I like doing different things. I've groomed dogs, ran a shipping department, worked at the Knox Mill."

"How important is education?"

"I wanted my children to complete school, but you don't need a college degree to get what you want out of life. It's harder just to find out what you really want to do. Very few around here like what they're doing—they call it a rat race. I see some of the nurses—they quit and start working at MBNA. I ask them how they like it, and they just say that the money's better. It didn't make them happier."

"So you're perfectly happy in your work and your life?"

"I like Maine, and there's a lot to see around here. Imagine—Tripper never went down to the breakwater [in Rockland]. I guess he was always busy with work, the kids, being married."

"Is there something missing in *your* life?"

"No. I love to read, all sorts of subjects. I never wanted to be a teacher, a nurse. I do like meeting different people. Maybe I'm just thinking I should be finding something, and there's nothing out there."

"Yet, you say you're more satisfied and happy than most of your co-workers."

"Maybe getting married so early had something to do with it. I had my son when I was fourteen. I've been divorced for thirteen years."

"You had to grow up fast. Maybe you thought you missed something, even if you didn't."

"I grew up with my kids, and I enjoyed that aspect, but it wasn't until my early thirties when I could have an evening to myself and do things totally on my own. Now the grandkids visit."

It seemed as if this woman, Dale, had lived a lifetime in her more than forty years. Maybe there isn't anything she missed.

◆   ◆   ◆

Dwinal and Dale find happiness picking up the trash in Bill's old truck. Some of us might tell ourselves that we wish we could be happy doing something like that. One temptation, of course, might be to become a creative trash collector and devise a system that would become so efficient it could be applied to other communities. More trucks could be purchased, and the business could evolve into one that shows us to be the great innovators of trash with one of the largest trash collecting businesses in the state. How's that for an accomplishment? Of course, we, unfortunately, would have to force Dwiny out of business by default, but he can always find another job somewhere, we think, maybe even work for us. That's the way it goes. Only, that *is* the way it goes. But where did *our* happiness go?

Now we walk uphill to the Common and bear to the right past the Cricket.

6

The Very Same Valentine

Next to the bed and breakfast on the Common, we come to what some old timers still call the Blacksmith's Shop. For many years the shop sat vacant, then it was used as an antique store for a number of years, but now Jim Ianello has totally remodeled it as Sterlingtown Realty.

Union was once known as Sterlingtown and also Taylor Town. Before I arrived in Union, I lived for a year in a Maine town named after someone. In Maine, it is always possible that people of a town's name still live there and have influence in the town. I made sure Union wasn't named after a Horatio Union, or some such. As it happens, Union was named because the people in the community pulled together.

Jim Ianello attended high school in Somerville, Massachusetts, and when he graduated from Tufts University in Boston, he was a trained electrical engineer. I remember when he purchased the building that houses his business and began remodeling it himself nearly two years ago. Now, a desk for an additional agent sits in one corner of the main room, but the walls remain unfinished and an array of photos of Union and houses for sale adorns one wall. A small stove pumps out heat.

I wanted to know the path that led him to real estate. "How did you see your possibilities in life while you were in high school?" I asked him.

"I knew I wanted to be an engineer. In the mid-sixties, NASA was planning a division in Cambridge, and that really appealed to me. I had a knack for electronics, and even in high school I was repairing TVs for people and fixing hi-fis." Jim, near middle age, with a solid body, a round face and dark curly hair, has an appealing earnestness that adds to his sense of the genuine. He was leaning back comfortably in his office desk chair, hands clasped behind his head.

"Did you enter the space program?"

"NASA never did come to Cambridge, but the summer before I entered college I got a great job working at Mass. General Hospital as an electronics technician. Even after I got my engineering degree, I continued to work in their computer science program as an engineer. I loved the stimulating environment, and I was single, and it was right downtown Boston."

"Why did you leave?"

"After fifteen years of it, it was no longer a challenge, and I was seduced into a sales job to sell electronic instrumentation. I became a sales rep."

"What was it about the offer that seduced you?"

"The increased freedom and the potential for income."

"Have those characteristics remained your primary motivating factor extending into your job here?"

He paused. "Yes. I had knowledge of the product with my training and experience in electronics. The same with this job. My knowledge of construction helps a great deal."

"You gotta know the territory," I said. Jim apparently did not have his mind on the *Music Man*, as I seem to always have with this book. He ignored my comment. "What happened then?" I asked him.

"After three years I got married—that was 1985—and we wanted to leave Boston and have a family. In fact, we were looking for a piece of vacation property in Maine, and after thinking about it, we decided to live in vacationland instead. Why not?"

"Then you got into real estate?"

"Even while I was in Mass., I began taking real estate courses in Maine. I knew about construction of homes, and with my sales experience, I felt that it would be a good fit."

"But you wanted to stay in sales. Why sales?"

He thought for a moment. "It wasn't sales as I had experienced previously, where you have a product and known competition, and you push your product and downplay the others. It wasn't off the shelf competition. In real estate, each sale is unique. You provide service."

"So you got a job in real estate in Maine?"

"In the period 1986-7 the real estate market was flying, but when I joined a firm in Maine, the market took a nosedive. That was 1988."

"Then what did you do?"

"I tried to make furniture for a living. I found that it was too much work for too little pay. So I approached a bank that needed a mortgage officer. They gave me the job, and I ended up selling their repossessed real estate. I sold all they had, and I sold myself out of a job—no other reason to work for a bank."

"That's where the money is," I chipped in. Jim grunted.

"Then what?"

"The real estate market was taking off again, and I took a job in commercial real estate. I worked for seven years in that. Now I have my own business." He gestured around him.

"When you have an idea that eventually changes your life—such as moving to Maine—how does that idea come about?"

"That's a long-term process. It took two years while we toyed with it. I thought it out carefully."

"What was the deciding factor?"

"If we didn't do it then, we would have had regrets, and we didn't want that, either. Besides, if it didn't work out, we could always move back to the Massachusetts scene."

"After making the decision, have your expectations been born out?"

He exhaled. "Everything—except for the financial. It's difficult to make a living in Maine. Difficult even with a lifestyle that's not extravagant. In this business, you need to be open to opportunity. If opportunity passes you by, then you lose money. Before, Kathy was with the kids while they were young. That impacted our income. Now she's teaching school in Warren."

"Do you need more business?"

"I can always use more listings," he said, "and the business is out there. It's frustrating that I haven't yet met one of my goals—to reach a level of critical mass in this office."

"Nuclear fission?"

"Not quite. But I have one other person in this office right now, and I am in the process of bringing on more. A group of agents who are connected to the community feed off one another, not exactly a feeding frenzy, but it's an atmosphere conducive to business."

"Why do you feel frustrated?"

"I need to finish this office and add desks, and also, it's difficult to attract experienced agents to Union."

"Why is that?"

"People want to live in Union because it's unspoiled and less hectic, but anyone working as a broker wants as much activity as possible, and that's why brokers want to work on the coast."

"What kind of person are you looking for?"

"Somebody who knows the ropes and is tied to the community, because this largely is a word-of-mouth business. People list with people who they know. The successful people that I know are those involved in business in the community and *then* decide to go into real estate."

"Has your work reflected, in any way, deeper aspects within you regarding service?"

"My work is a 'matching' service—matching people to their homes. There's really little or no sales involved. It's an adventure, like any sales company, but I'm careful not to do the hard sell—but all the time being attentive to the clients. People need time to imagine themselves in a new place. They don't want to listen to a hard sell."

"So how do you sell to them?"

"I basically respond to them. I present all the possibilities." Jim held up a small packet of paper. I could see colored pictures and paragraphs of typing. "Here's all the property for sale in Union. I'm giving it to a client this morning. I have the tools. I present the choices. I show price versus value. I don't push."

"Does this reflect personal values?"

"One of the values I have is that I appreciate someone respecting me enough to allow me to make my own decisions."

"There's got to be some sales involved," I said. "Don't you accentuate the positive?"

"This is *not* a customer, but a *client*," he said, firmly. "I have a legal responsibility to make the client aware of the negatives. The positives are usually obvious."

"Where is the 'sales'?"

"This job does not fulfill the criteria as a sales job. Hype is inappropriate. This is not selling cars. I provide the data so clients can make their own decisions. As a consumer myself, I always do lots of research to get as much information as I can before I buy, say, a car. I assume everyone wants to make informed decisions."

"This is very pragmatic behavior—using reason to make decisions, with an added dollop of humanism," I said.

"I hate irrationality," he said.

"Passion is losing oneself into emotion," I said. "Do you ever give into emotion?"

He gave me a tight smile. "I suppose I ought to."

"What do you mean?"

"Some people think impulsiveness is an attribute," he replied, and then he exhaled. "But that isn't consistent with my personality."

"You work to facilitate the process of people seeking to make major decisions: to buy property, homes. You present the choices, allowing people to make up their own minds. You help people make free choices. Is this the fulfilling part of your job?"

"I feel most fulfilled when a sale is closed and both parties are happy. Then they can move on. I like helping people. Many other elements in the job are like any other job—including moments of high anxiety. Interpersonal relationships give me enjoyment, and I like being part of a larger network of realtors—having a common interest."

"Yet you are alone here on the Common doing what you do. Do you feel alone?"

"Not in a negative sense. I want to be one of the few 'kids on the block' when the growth comes. Growth *is* coming."

"You move here to get away from what growth brings, and you now want to capitalize on that growth. That seems like a paradox."

"Rather than fight it, I've become part of the fabric of this community. I have lots of friends here now. It will be years before this place is as intolerable as Camden."

"Does religion or philosophy have anything to do with your role in your job?"

"I see religion and philosophy as one. I try to operate with honesty, be trustworthy, and I have complete respect for anyone I deal with. I have no greater respect for a millionaire than someone just scraping by."

"Don't you think that if a person with lots of money came in here and wanted to buy an expensive house, wouldn't that turn your head a bit?"

"It doesn't turn my head if a person is looking at a high price range, as opposed to a person walking into here looking for a mobile home. The chance of success is less with a person who has money. A sale is a sale. I'm just as anxious to list a mobile home as a $350,000 house. A sale is a sale."

"Then in your business, success equals sales?"

"Yes. Transactions equal success."

"Is there any other gauge of success for you in this business other than transactions?"

"No. But I don't know what else there might be."

"Just that some people have other religious or philosophical agendas in their business, other than the end result, which is a transaction."

"Not with me," he said.

"What kinds of things might you do to facilitate a transaction if you think either of the parties is distressed because of the terms, or because they can't quite afford it?"

"It's amazing to me how little things will make or break a deal. For instance, something as trivial as a woodstove, or a refrigerator—both very small items when compared to the price of a house."

"What do you mean?"

"It's that irrational behavior that I hate so much. They want to know if the refrigerator is included in the final price, and if it isn't, then the deal is off. It doesn't make any sense. Or sometimes, if I surrender $200 or $500 on the commission, that will make the deal go through."

"Sounds like car sales," I said. "Is this irrationality the most frustrating part of your work?"

"No. The most frustrating—maybe I should say most unnerving part—is not knowing what the future holds, because of the variability of the market. A broker needs operating capital, and I get nervous when times start to turn bad. I'm conservative by nature regarding spending, but the economy can stifle any plans that I have for growth in the business."

"That's why the place is not finished?"

He nodded. "I have a friend who works for the telephone company, and he tells me that he always knows when a new business is not going to last. They are the ones who want the most expensive equipment. I don't believe in reckless spending."

"Do you get fed up with the whole thing sometimes?"

"No, but sometimes I feel a panic, and then I scramble to finish something—maybe it's a wiring job around here—rather than succumb to a defeatist attitude. I'm an accomplishment sort of guy, and completing a project puts something else behind me. That helps, because I always have a big 'to do' list."

"How about a vacation?"

"I don't have sufficient backup to take my mind off work more than a week. We did go to Moosehead for a week last summer."

"Can you tell me what it is in you that allows you to work by and for yourself as opposed to working for someone else, in a group?"

"I never considered myself a businessman until these last couple of years. I am not a risk taker at all. It is just that I reached a point where I felt I had enough knowledge that I could do this job—that I knew what I was doing. Before, I didn't know enough."

"Is that what stops other people from going into business on their own?"

"I think it's complacency, inertia, and, believe it or not—health insurance. I think a lot of people would make good entrepreneurs, except for the health insurance crisis. We're fortunate because Kathy gets good insurance from her work at school."

"Does fear play a part in your life?"

"Yes—major—the fear of over-extending myself. It's a preoccupation."

"Does it affect your health?"

"I guess not, because I'm healthy."

"That must indicate that this job is a good fit. Did you have to plan much before you started this business?"

"I put a lot of thought into this—two years—but what triggered it was this building. I didn't decide to have a business and then buy a building. It was the other way around. I could visualize this as my real estate office. First I visualize, then I execute a plan, step by step."

"Is the first step in your creative process to visualize?"

"Yes. I have been given the ability to visualize."

"Pictures?"

"Yes. That's the only way I can think."

I pointed to a portable radio sitting on the windowsill. "Can you take that radio apart in your mind, step by step?"

"Yes," he replied.

"In full color?" He nodded. I was impressed.

"I'll bet you dream in full color, too." He nodded again. "Do you hear anything when you plan in pictures?"

"Probably me talking to myself."

"Were you always like this—having this ability to visualize?"

"I remember being artistic as a child. I could draw, paint."

"Have you ever known anyone that could visualize as you do?"

"I never had this conversation before," he replied.

"Your visualization ability must have been of great value in engineering. I'm surprised you didn't invent things."

"I did. While I was working for Mass. General, I invented a phone dialer for computers. It was great fun."

"Why didn't you just keep going in engineering, inventing and creating?"

"I guess I needed my work attached to personal relationships. In engineering, you deal with things. I believe the most important thing in life is interpersonal relationship—family and friends."

"Is the rest of your family like that?"

"My older sister is a social person—loves life. Because of the way she treats others, she enjoys others, and life."

"Were your parents like that?"

"Yes, an Italian family—very family-oriented."

"So, is this your ideal job?"

"If I could make money with my hands, I would do it. I tried to make furniture for a living, but that can be pretty isolating. To tell you the truth, I've found, through experience, that the people in this world who are the happiest are the people who enjoy other humans."

"You're a pragmatic humanist, but you also need to create."

He gestured around him. "The building, the presentation—everything. Business is a creation."

The phone rang. Another customer. I knew my way out.

◆   ◆   ◆

I interviewed Kathy, Jim's wife, at their home. We sat in a well windowed, open-beamed room at a harvest table made by Jim. Kathy has the positive presence of a good teacher and the sort of fair complexion and red hair that self-selects to a northern clime.

After graduation from college in Massachusetts, Kathy earned a master's degree in early childhood education and then went on to further graduate work at Harvard. Later, she worked at the Department of Education in Massachusetts. By the time she and Jim married and moved to Maine, they had one child, and their second boy was soon to arrive. She became a stay-at-home mom. Now that one of the boys is in college and the other in high school, she is teaching special education at the elementary school in Warren, bordering Union.

"What was it like moving to Maine?" I asked her.

"We found ourselves making new friends, valued new friends, and we found that we had a lot in common with them—people willing to take the risk in coming here. It was something intangible that attracted us together."

"Did you find that you mostly made friends with people 'from away'?"

"I think you're right."

"Why Maine?"

"I grew up in a small community in New Hampshire, and we didn't lock our doors. Boston was different, and it was wearing on Jim. We took to the rural life."

"What were your goals along that line?"

"We wanted a nice house, and more than a few acres. My goal was to do part-time consultant work, and Jimmy's was to work for himself. He wanted to do woodworking."

"How did that play out?"

"I didn't know how much trouble it was going to be to find consultant work. At the same time, Jim was doing mostly custom woodwork, and he didn't enjoy that, because it lacked the creative element, and a few times, he got burned doing exactly what the customers wanted, and then they changed their mind. He can make beautiful furniture, but he had to make what he could sell. Then our own house needed work. It was a difficult time."

"So Jim is selling real estate on his own now. Do you see that as a sales job?"

"The thing with Jimmy is that he is so trustworthy. People see him as a friend—customers end up being friends—and he serves as an advisor, because he can help them, especially since he knows about construction. I have a lot of respect for him. He helps the people, and sometimes he doesn't get paid for that. He loves working on his building, too, and being part of the community—people stopping by to talk."

"Does religion or philosophy play a big part in your lives?"

"Jimmy was brought up in an Italian Catholic family, most of them are very close, not that we go to church. I was raised in the Congregational Church. We were married in the Congregational Church, and later we attended the local Methodist Church so the boys could go to Sunday school." [The closest Catholic Church is sixteen miles away in Rockland.]

"Jim says that in real estate, a sale is a sale to him. Philosophically, is there more to it than that?"

She pondered for a moment. "Most of all, I think, he values being fair. I know that he gives leads to other brokers. He has good relations with Rick Whelan [the other broker with a Union office]. When I first met him he was selling electronic equipment, and he would not make a sale at someone else's expense. He found that unattractive in other salespeople."

"He says that fear of over-extension in business plays a big part in his life. How do you see that?"

"I am aware of it. On the one hand, I'm glad that he's conscientious. He's smart and careful about money. His mother is like that. It was instilled in him, though he has some friends that aren't like that at all, and they max out all their credit cards."

"He can visualize things. What does that add or not add to the relationship?"

"He can visualize things, but I'm not sure he can always articulate what he is seeing. Sometimes I have a hard time seeing what he is seeing, and we might have an argument, because we are not on the same page. Mostly, I've learned to trust his visualization."

"You two seem to have a 50/50 relationship. What are the things that you bring into the relationship?"

"Before I worked full-time, he relied on me for the kids, keeping the home together. Now he relies on me for a steady income and benefits. But throughout it all, we rely on each other for feedback on anything we're feeling or worrying about."

"Ideas are the basis for changes in direction in people's lives," I said. "How do you access ideas?"

"I'll have ideas about the kids, and that would get the discussion going. He'll have ideas about the house, car, money—he's always thinking about the money part."

"Do either of you use a process of meditation, quiet thought, or prayer to find new directions?"

"Nearly always we are driven by practical matters when we are faced with a problem. We talk about it, and then if there's no solution, we talk some more, maybe wait a while, but we don't need to take time out, like in meditation. We need to negotiate, see both perspectives, discuss all our options and give it time. Amazingly, we seem to come to the same conclusions at the same time."

"Many people cannot do what you do. What do you think is the difference?"

"One thing is that we are not attached to things. For instance, we've done a lot of work on this house, but I would easily sell it and move to another, or another. We're not attached to or defined by our possessions."

"That sounds Eastern," I said. "Have you further defined your religious or philosophical belief system?"

"Funny you would ask that, because I have just been having discussions with Tom, who's a senior in high school, and he is studying belief systems. When I was still in high school I started voicing my concerns about our traditional beliefs, and I think my mother was kind of hurt, but I believed I was right. Later in college, I thought more about it, but I found *not* many people who had those views, too. I felt alone. Jim and I, of course, have talked about it. He is very open to the possibilities of other belief systems. We went ahead with our lives together, anyway."

"Religious thought has been around as long as man," I said. "So, there exists a completely thought out religious system for any set of beliefs. Have you found such a system?"

"I haven't looked that hard. We have so many other things that take precedence in our lives. I've had inklings what it might be, and it has something to do with looking forward and including newer thinking and possibilities."

"Your life with Jim seems to march forward with your commonality of philosophy, regardless of the religious difference," I said.

"He feels that he would like to be doing more in his religion, but, like me, he has so many other things going on. It's not a priority at this time. I suppose a lot of married couples are like we are. I'll frequently say something and he'll say that he was thinking the very same thing—and this Valentine's Day, we gave each other the very same valentine. Funny."

◆   ◆   ◆

You may have been impressed, as was I, that Jim and Kathy's relationship combines both head and heart. We see rationality along with basic compatibility, but also personal qualities that complement one another. This is an eclectic relationship with elements entering from different angles: humanism, rationality, creativity, a lack of attachment to possessions, commitment to service and fairness, the intuitive quality of vision and the acceptance of diversity, as Jim and Kathy overstep religious difference. There is a little of Romeo and Juliet here, too, but without the tragedy. Instead of creating a foundation for themselves on religion and all the divisiveness that could surface with those differences, Jim and Kathy face the problems in their everyday world with the confidence of reason and love.

Jim's approach to his business and Gary Sukeforth's approach sound nearly identical with their ideas of service and fairness. The only difference is that Jim has the support of Kathy, his loyal wife, whereas Gary is unmarried. Advantages exist for both.

Just next door to Sterlingtown Realty is Ken Rogers' place. Let us see what he is doing.

7

Time Out

Ken Rogers' shop sits between the post office and Jim Ianello's real estate office. Ken's shop was, for many years, a gasoline station; and before that, a livery stable. Although the gas pumps were pulled out, there is still the look of a 1950s service station, with two large service doors and a small adjacent office space.

The garage space is now a clean, well-lighted and equipped auto trim shop in which sits a 1950 Plymouth convertible with the entire insides gutted and its exterior re-welded and molded—the metal shining from sanding. Beside it rests a '53 Ford Prefect in the process of renewal.

The small reception area, upon entering the front door, has pictures of cars that Ken has redone. One of the "before" pictures, painted by Ken's former wife, is of an abandoned car, rusted and surrounded by weeds. Ken's former wife also created the painting used in the design on the cover of my last book.

Ken had come to Union in 1987. Up until a few years ago, he lived near the Common a couple of houses away from Frank Austin. Behind Ken's house sat an old building that once was a creamery. Ken was in the process of refurbishing the creamery to be his shop when the divorce interceded, and he moved into his shop on the Common. He has since sold his old house. On the other side of the Common many years ago, there was a carriage shop. Ken's establishment, in my mind, carries on that tradition.

"What did you do when you first came to Union?" I asked him.

"I worked in Massachusetts installing auto restyling packages. We worked mostly with new car dealers. I had been coming to Maine on and off since I was young. I wanted to have my own place, and I didn't think anyone was doing that kind of work here." He snuffed out his cigarette. Ken, sharp featured from gauntness, has a body small enough to allow him to squirm around the recesses of an automobile.

"Did you have success at first?"

"There wasn't much interest here in Maine. The first job I got was from a new car dealer, Linwood Moody, at Moody Pontiac in Rockland. I had to go to Mass. to get the materials. Then he gave me another job right off."

"Then did your business take off?"

"Gradually it increased, but there are cycles. I'm not that aggressive, either. It would have helped if I were more of a salesman type. I had to use the money I earned to buy the materials."

"What is it about cars?" I asked.

"I always liked cars, and I figured I would do what needed to be done with them. They're a big pain in the neck, but you can't live without them."

"Would you get as much satisfaction, let's say, in stylizing a car as you would if you fixed the car's engine for someone?"

"More with restyling."

"Why?"

"It shows more when it's done. My intent has always been to do it perfectly, to my ability, but I get a lot of jobs that I've never done, so there's stress, too. Old cars, new cars; each of them is different. Especially with the new cars; you just can't unscrew them apart."

"It must be difficult at times, when there isn't much work."

"That's when Howard will send me something. [Howard Stetson, owner of the Saab dealership in Warren, which is literally out in the middle of the country, about five miles from Union.] Howard's got me through some hard times. So did Richard Kirkpatrick—keeping me, my finances and a lot of other things going." [Richard lives in town.]

"But, still, it's difficult to plan. You don't know if you'll have enough money to go on."

"I go week-to-week. I always say that next year I'll be able to put some money away."

"It must be a real downer at times, when there's nothing going on."

"I don't worry about money. I'm a survivor. Money always seems to come when I need it. In fact, I hold back. I don't want to have a boom and all that business."

"How does a person get to the point that he's not overly concerned about money? Most people think about money much of the time."

"Probably the way I was brought up. We lived good and had lots of things, but my dad built all the stuff that we had, a swimming pool, a boat, even a rope-tow ski area out in back."

"What kind of business was he in?"

"He worked for the State [Massachusetts], and retired. I tried working like he did for the state, but I didn't want to be in an office all day." Ken lit a cigarette.

"What kind of life did you have in mind when you came to Maine?"

"I wanted this place, and it was for sale, and I wanted my own home, which I *had*. I like working on the Common. It's a good place to have a business. I've never had to give a person directions to get here, but I'm not crazy about living on the Common."

"Do you have any heroes in life?"

"I like Dale Ernhardt." [NASCAR driver.]

"What is it about automobiles? What's the appeal?"

"Having something unique. To have something that everyone else has, but make it different."

"What is the attraction in that?"

"Maybe to be recognized by someone, but that's just the opposite of what I am, myself. I'd just as soon not have people notice me. But I've always liked a nice car. What would people think if I drove a beat up old VW—me being in the kind of business that I'm in?" [Ken drives a shiny green pickup.]

"You must have liked cars when you were young."

"I used to draw cars all the time. I couldn't wait to get my license. What is it you're writing about, anyway? Why is this important?"

I explained to him, briefly, how I think that men who both live and work in a well-defined community like Union demonstrate a synthesis of what is salvageable in the philosophic currents of the day. People are living philosophy, I said, and they do what they believe in, even though they might not put it all into words. I was interested in grassroots philosophy—what people actually lived. With that, he seemed satisfied, in fact, encouraged to go on.

"It's different," I said "than if you lived in Union and worked, say, at MBNA in Belfast."

"Yeah," he replied, "those people have a steady income. But I could do more. I could do airplane seats, interiors—whatever. My kids are getting interested in working here. With them, I might get into some of that business."

"It has all the ingredients for a family business," I said.

"I've got the family [he has three children]. Not many jobs out there. They've been looking."

"You live on the Common and work on the Common. What are your relations with other store owners here?"

"We all seem to stay in our own areas. I talk to them, but I don't really talk with them."

"If you had to do this all over again, would you do the same?"

"I think so. I still like doing what I do."

"One more time, I want to ask what the appeal of fixing up cars is for you. What is it like?"

"It's a before and after thing. You take something that looks no good, but after you finish it, it looks brand new again. I have cars—like that Plymouth out there—with nothing in them, and I have to design a whole new thing, and then figure out how to do it."

"I can see where that would be satisfying. I see a computer system and a digital camera over there. How do you use those devices?"

"I recommend books—car repair and restoration books, especially for old cars on my Web site, KARonline.com. Then, if anyone ends up buying one of the books, I get a commission. That's what I like about the Internet. If I can figure out how to double what I'm doing now, and then double that, I would be set." He nodded toward the camera. "I been fooling around with the digital camera. I take pictures of things having to do with cars—modify them with techniques."

"You aren't very traditional," I said.

"I'm always thinking of different ways to make ends meet by looking for the new. I've never had much schooling; so it's tough sometimes to figure things out, but I do. I figure if someone else can do a thing, then I can do it, too."

"Where did the educational system and you part ways?"

"I ran away from home when I was fifteen, and I skipped school. So they kicked me out."

"They kicked you out because you skipped school?" I exclaimed. Ken nodded, as we both laughed at the irony of it all.

"What did you do then?"

"I went to work at a car wash—my first job."

"Would you have stayed in school if they had let you?"

"I didn't want that stuff on me. But I did get my GED later, and I've gone back to school for things I wanted, like drafting and flying."

"What was it about school?"

"The routine. Everyday. Having to get up—be there early. Alarm clocks."

"Time limits don't fit well with a lot of humans," I said. "What else was it about school?"

"I know I didn't like school, and my grades showed it. I was bored with it. You should be allowed to go to school when you want to, when you know what you want. I did fine when it was something I wanted. Like in history, I couldn't understand why we had to know about the presidents and all those dates. But now, the History Channel is my favorite channel. It's more interesting now."

"It seems ironic to me that you live here on the Common, and when you look out your window, you see a Civil War statue yet, you are what I would call innovative, not traditional. You use innovation in your work all the time."

"I don't throw away anything. Upstairs is full of stuff. This table here, I got the wood from the old creamery behind my house."

"You use innovation to figure out ways to survive."

"To make things better," he replied. "Any extra money I put back into the shop, but I don't think it's all about work. Free time is just as important as money."

"Do you enjoy your customers? Or are people who want you to fix up their cars a difficult and demanding sort?"

"I've had little trouble because they're into cars, too, and they want something nice."

"So you share your love of cars with your customers. Is that a true statement?" Ken nodded in the affirmative. "Then, after that, there isn't much more to say," I remarked.

Ken shook his head and managed a smile.

◆   ◆   ◆

We would do well to talk with Richard Kirkpatrick, Ken's close friend. To talk with Richard we have to leave the village center and travel east on Route 17 a short distance.

Richard Kirkpatrick was my first patient when I arrived in Union in 1972. I remember him coming by, unannounced, into the kitchen and talking to me while he leaned his arm on our old Philco refrigerator. I forget what it was about, and I think I wrote him out a prescription. When he was set to leave, he asked me about payment. I told him it wasn't enough for there to be a charge. From then on, whenever I saw Richard as a patient, I couldn't seem to get around to asking him to pay for anything, perhaps because he was my first patient. It wasn't that he couldn't pay, but for some reason, I didn't seem to want to ask him to pay.

Richard is a jack-of-all-trades and, he says, a master of none. However, over the last thirty years or so, he has done a lot for our family, and it's always a battle to get him to bill us. He slips in to fix an appliance or unclog a septic line and maybe we'll get a bill—especially if he had to buy parts or spend a lot of time—and maybe we won't. Richard is not this way only with our family, but it is his standard fare in this town. If anyone calls for help and it's urgent, Richard will be at the door that morning. If it's not urgent, then one day he will show up at your door or he will already be working in your cellar when you return home.

Once he clamps onto a job, Richard sticks with it to the bitter end. He worked well into the night on a water well problem that we once had. Such persistence pervades this community, as well as others in Maine. I imagine it would be difficult fighting these Maine men in a war. These tenacious men would not ease up on the enemy, not back down. What an awful war the Civil War must have been. We have our Civil War statue on the Common, as do most of the communities in Maine. Union had 160 men lost in that war, and 158 in World War II.

At Union's Founders Day, held on the Common every year, townspeople arrive to hear a band in the bandstand (the gazebo), eat chicken barbecue, peruse the crafts tables and listen to a few presentations. Nothing fancy, everyone wears whatever he or she feels like wearing according to what the weather dictates—weather remains the dictator around here. At one Founders Day, people were milling about when the presenter asked the Vietnam veterans to stand before the crowd. I saw Richard approach and a few others, and I thought, Well, I was in Vietnam—and I considered not joining the others, given that I had done what I was required I do. Then I asked myself, Why not? So, I stood in a small assemblage facing the audience with an odd feeling in my stomach.

While in the service, Richard was stationed in California where he met his first wife. She returned to Maine with him, and they had a girl and two boys. One of the boys works at the farm machinery equipment place on Route 17, and the other is a teacher and helps Richard during the summer.

Richard mows fifty lawns, including all the cemeteries and the Common during the summer, and he does repair services year-round, but especially during the winter. Richard is wiry and muscular, has a ruddy complexion with a bush of curly hair and he usually sports a short beard. He grew up on a dairy farm in Union, and his family goes back generations in Maine.

For the interview with Richard, we were sitting in the cellar of his split-level home, comfortable in a couple of old upholstered chairs, surrounded by stuff for storage. I asked him about his work, and I said that his job was different from what most people do.

"I love it," he robustly replied. "I like being my own boss. I've worked for people before, and I had to get up and punch in. That's not for me."

"A lot of young men in Maine go away and they don't come back. Why did you come back?"

"Put it this way," he said, "places I went to, I really didn't like. I like the four seasons. I like home."

"It's all word-of-mouth. I never see you advertise. How do you get work?"

"Put it this way, go check all my messages. I do call 'em all back, but it might be a while before I get to it. I'm a workaholic. Have to survive in this world. I'm making a good living. I'm happy, and I've a nice wife—that's the big part."

"You seem to have everything you need," I said.

"Why would I want to do anything different than this?" he replied.

◆   ◆   ◆

Short and sweet, that's what it's all about with Richard. Ken and Richard are good friends, and they have quite a lot in common doing their own things in their work, no timetables and working within the community of Union. One big difference exists between them, however. While Ken is relatively new to Maine, Richard has deep roots in the community. Richard knows everyone and knows what's going on about town. Every newcomer needs a friend like Richard.

It's a bit difficult breaking into a small community at first. Patterns exist and people look at a newcomer with the suspicion that he or she will try to change the ways of the community, or that they will stay just long enough to stir things up, and then move away. Why invest in someone who will likely move away? It's not so easy living in Maine. To survive, people usually work at more than one job, and individuals need to know—or learn—how to fix many things on their own.

Initially, I was as weird as any newcomer was. Shortly after meeting Richard more than thirty years ago, I asked him to deliver a couple of cords of firewood, because we had a woodstove, though we didn't have a woodlot at that time. Richard and his father had cut the wood, and Richard trucked it over and dumped it in our dooryard. He helped me to stack it, and later I told him that I thought the wood wasn't very good because some of it was alder.

"None of that wood is alder," Richard retorted.

Was any of it alder? No. None of it was. I had just learned what alder *was*, and I guess I was trying to show that I knew the different kinds of wood—but I did not—not at that time. Why did I say what I did? It was ignorant, but I'm guessing that Richard merely shrugged his shoulders and muttered something to himself about newcomers as he went on his way.

I eventually married into Maine, which allowed me the opportunity to have roots here. My wife, Dianne, is from Jefferson, a couple of towns over from Union. A newcomer to Maine often socializes with other people from out of state, as did Jim and Kathy Ianello when they arrived in Maine. However, by marrying into a family from within the state, a person becomes a part of that family by default and therefore is considered to have roots here—and most everything changes. A large difference exists between newcomers who have raised their children in the state and those who have not. In the first instance, the children will have the opportunity to be "real" Mainers. You are considered a Mainer by Mainers when you have family roots; otherwise, you are viewed as "from away."

I became initiated into Union shortly after I arrived in town. One day, Pudgy (Frank Austin's father-in-law), the attendant at the Union dump, tapped on my door and soundly told me that I was not to dump my trash outside the gate of the dump just because the dump happened to be closed. True, I had been to the dump, once, and I did drop off some trash, but I threw it on the dump.

He took a rumpled snippet of paper from his coat pocket and squinted at the writing. "You're the new doc, right?"

I said that I guessed I was.

"Then you dumped the trash, like I said." He handed me the paper. "That's your name, I believe. I took it off an envelope."

Written on the paper in pencil was the name of a doctor, but it wasn't me. It turned out that the doctor was a psychologist, and he was new to the area, too.

Pudgy wasn't too happy that he had to go elsewhere to find the doctor who was fool enough to dump his trash outside the dump gates. Strains of Alice's Restaurant ran through my head.

Pudgy, the icon of the dump, tragically died some years later, burned to death slipping down the incline of trash and into the fire.

◆   ◆   ◆

To end the interviews of this chapter, I will jump to the younger generation and speak with Ken Rogers' fifteen-year-old daughter, Chelsea, now a sophomore in the Camden/Rockport school system on the coast. Chelsea lives in Appleton with her mother, who has remarried. Chelsea is small, with beautifully delicate features and a soft voice. Her dad brought Chelsea straight from school to his shop today. I asked her about her high school experience.

"I didn't like it. I didn't feel it was the place for me—until I finally got into alternative school."

"What is the alternative school?"

"It's a place for kids if they learn differently than the traditional way. Most of the kids there wanted to drop out when they went to high school. It's a chance to learn what you want to."

"What interests you?"

"Photography and cars."

"If many of the kids want to learn many different things, how do just a few teachers do that?"

"They have what they call community connections, and they find someone who does the thing in the community that the student wants to do."

"How did you come about getting into the alternative school?"

"I didn't have many friends, and I couldn't function because I didn't see myself as academically smart. I felt I had better things to do, and I was falling behind. There's a lot of money in that high school, and I felt out of place."

"Have you changed your opinion of yourself?"

"I'm doing better in school, and I now have friends who like me for who I am. That's good, and it took me until this year to find these people."

"How does the future look to you?"

"I want to go to Florida and work down there, and later maybe do something in photography, having to do with cars, but not necessarily what my dad does."

Chelsea is referring to her two older brothers who work in Florida in a seasonal resort, both of whom went there after high school. Chelsea's brothers are some of the "Boca boys" that Rich Wiemer referred to in his interview in Chapter Two.

"What do you think of what your dad does?"

"You don't see his type of business around. He does things that I don't even know how he does them—covering seats, doing designs, and it takes him a long time to do it. I have a lot of respect for his work."

"What is it about cars?" I asked.

"I was always curious about them, and both of my brothers love them."

"What is it about Boca?"

"Mainly, I want to be with my brothers."

"Are you going to leave school to be with them?"

"No, I'm going to graduate."

"Do you see yourself as being as happy as other kids your age?"

"Not really."

"What's missing?"

"I miss two of my friends, and my uncle. They all died."

I felt a pall around me, a dark cloak in the room.

"How did they die?"

"One committed suicide, and the other died in a boating accident. My uncle died of a heart attack."

It suddenly dawned on me that I knew the stories of the boys to whom Chelsea was referring. One boy attended the Medomak Valley High School. He reportedly said goodbye to his friends one day at school, and later that same day in his own home, he hung himself. The other boy was planning to return to the same school but was working on a fishing trawler that mysteriously disappeared, all hands lost. With other kids their age, these two boys and Chelsea spent time skateboarding at the Methodist church parking lot just below Union's post office. The first boy died during Chelsea's freshman year, then her uncle died and finally the fishing boat disappeared, all in a period of six months, the last one in October just as she was beginning the alternative school in her current school year.

I asked her what her state of mind was just before all this began to happen.

"I was depressed, anyway. Nothing was going right. I was missing a lot of school, failing all my classes."

"Then the suicide. What happened to you after?"

"I got ten times worse, but I also opened up to my mother, which was a first."

"Is that channel still open?"

"Yes," she replied.

"Describe to me what your life was like."

"Everything didn't go right—it just kept getting worse."

"Can you describe your state of mind with one word?"

She thought for a while, and given a list of possibilities, she chose, "Hopeless."

"Did you consider suicide?"

"No."

"Why not?"

"I saw what it did to me and everyone else."

"To have come to that very mature realization, did you have to think of suicide yourself at all?"

"I did think of it, very briefly, but then I thought of all the people left behind, and I decided to not even go there."

"It sounds as if you have to at least consider it before you can reject it. Is that correct?"

She nodded a yes.

"Then your uncle died. Did the experience you had just come through help you in any way with your uncle's death?"

"No. I kept heading down. That was at the end of the year, but I started going back to school, because I didn't want to be a freshman again."

"Then the fishing accident," I said.

"Same thing," she replied. "It hit me hard."

"You were starting in the alternative school and getting your feet on the ground. What happened then?"

"I started missing school, but one thing: I kept a journal with one of my teachers, and she would respond by writing a paragraph or a page after I wrote. That helped me a lot. And my mother's involvement. That helped."

"How about your father?"

"I don't think he knew what to say."

"It's been four months now since the last of all that, how are you doing now?"

"I'm actually going to school. I still have my days, but I'm happy for the most part."

"Do you think that you are a person who will be bothered by depression later in your life?"

"I have it, on and off."

"How do you look at it?"

"I never really looked at it. It's not fun."

"Did anyone ever suggest medicine?"

"Yes, but medicine sugar coats a thing. It doesn't really fix it."

"Is this something that you believe you will overcome?"

"I think I will figure out ways. Otherwise, I guess I'll just have to put up with it."

"Have you talked with other people like you who have depression?"

"No, not really."

"If there were a group of other young people that had depression, would you take the time to talk with them, as part of a group?"

She smiled and shook her head. "No, I can handle it myself."

"Do you feel alone, that there is no one else like you?"

"Yes, kinda."

"If you had a choice, and you thought that depression was a problem, would you say that the cause of the problem is from life in general, or because of society being screwed up, or because of something the matter with the way you are put together? Which would you think?

"Life."

"Have you been exposed to religion?"

"I was exposed a lot when I was growing up in Union. I'm not against it, and I don't hate it, but I'm not really religious."

"Can you be different and still be accepted in your present life?"

"It all depends. I know people who are very different, and they still have friends."

"So the key is being able to find those you can relate to?"

"Yes."

"With a peer group, do you still feel alone?"

"The peer group is social," she said.

"You have a boyfriend," I said. "I have seen you kiss him in front of the shop. Does being with him help you not feel so alone?"

"It takes it away a little, but it's still there. Having him around makes me feel happier."

"The feeling of being alone—would you want to continue in life even if you thought that feeling would always be there?"

"Yes, I think…sort of."

"Do you think you have courage?"

"Yes," she said.

I agreed.

◆   ◆   ◆

In a recent *Scientific American*, [Vol. 287, n. 3] a poem written by Titus Maccius Plautus (b. 254 b.c.) is quoted on the subject of time:

> The gods confound the man
>
> who first found out
>
> How to distinguish hours.
>
> Confound him, too,
>
> Who in this place set up
>
> a sundial,
>
> To cut and hack
>
> my days so wretchedly
>
> Into small portions!

School begins the tyranny of the clock in earnest. We must be there at a particular time, and then school chops up the day into learning periods in which the clock, not interest, determines how long we spend at any particular endeavor. Time is exclusionary, because it contains any activity while it excludes others. We look on activities in terms of time, and with digital clocks, our timings have become even more exact.

Ken, Richard and Chelsea all have issues with time. Ken works at his own pace only on older cars. Those are cars not needed urgently for everyday transportation. Richard works according to the clients' needs, the more urgent, the sooner. Chelsea has found a non-traditional school that does not break up the day into immovable barriers of time. The more time becomes exact, then the more people it excludes, though some people thrive on the constraints of time. In our highly productive culture, can we blame the estrangement of so many people on their feelings of exclusion because of time?

The ultimate exclusionary move in life is suicide. In suicide, we suddenly exclude ourselves, and in so doing, we bring others into the act through guilt. The feelings of being alone or feeling rootless connect to thinking about suicide, especially in the young. I termed these feelings "exclusion."

Time certainly has something to do with exclusion. Does time have anything to do with suicide? I think that question needs an answer, sometime.

Next door to Ken's shop is the post office. Let us walk over and talk with Postmaster Mike Arbour.

8

Staying Put

The Union Post Office is a solid brick building with the Zip Code, 04862, on a small sign mounted in front. Not too many years ago, a sanatorium sat on this property with a breezeway connected to the livery stable that is now Ken Rogers' establishment. Mike Arbour has been the postmaster for nearly five years. For the first year, he commuted from Camden where he rented an apartment. Since working at the Union Post Office, he has purchased a house in town, married, and the couple now has two children. Mike has two older children from a previous marriage, but they mostly live in Augusta from where Mike used to commute to the post office in Camden. Before that, he commuted to many other Maine post offices, some at great distance, and all bigger than Union's.

After work and on weekends, I see Mike running on the road, pushing a three-wheeled cart containing his youngest daughter. From his stride, you know he is an athlete, broad shouldered and tall, a height he has passed on to his basketball star son. Usually he has a close-cropped beard to go with his close-cropped dark hair.

I asked Mike what the big difference was between commuting to work and living in the same town in which he worked.

"In Camden, I only rented," he replied. "That's not like owning a place in town and voting on local issues and being involved, having my heart there."

"What do you mean by 'heart'?"

"I lived in Camden—but I really didn't. If someone asked me where I lived, I had to think for a minute."

"So 'heart' means belonging?"

"Yes," he replied. "Belonging means owning—to have a commitment there."

"Sounds as if you were more like a visitor in Camden." I said

"Right, a visitor; but here, living and working in Union, first and foremost, there's more home time, less travel time. I can come home for lunch, have time with the kids, even mow the lawn. [Mike likes a trim lawn.]

"The other thing, from a working standpoint, there's more of a sense of pride. What I do has effects on everybody I see. If I see thirty faces at the grocery store, I know that I *serve* them, and I can put a *name* to a face with nearly all of them. I think it means more to them, too, having someone who lives right here. I don't intend to leave."

"Give me an example of how you might act if you worked in a town and had your 'heart' there and how you might act if you didn't."

"You want a roll of stamps? $37. Here..." He gestured as if handing me a roll of stamps. Then he looked beyond me, "Next...

"I didn't have a vested interest in your life," he said, "and there wasn't as much need for conversation—just going through the motions—and you won't take the time to get to know me, either. But regardless of where I work, there's a certain way my job has to be done, and if I can add a touch of humanity—maybe bring a smile to your face, or make light of something, even though that experience was brief, then it was a positive experience."

"So commitment is a big deal."

"Yes, absolutely—on a professional level."

"What do you mean—on a 'professional level'?"

"I want to do the right thing by the community. Being involved, it becomes a way of life. But there's a *line*. It's black and white when it comes to work and private life."

"Explain that."

"This weekend I'll be helping with a barn-raising. It's something that I want to do. But some people expect more from me just because of my job. If there's work to be done in the community, like at the dunking tank at the Fair. [The Union Fair is the town's single big annual event.] Because I'm postmaster and everybody knows me, if I say no, and I see the scowl on the other person's face, then all of a sudden I'm not the same guy that leaves them smiling. It takes them off guard—I don't like that part of it. Sometimes I feel guilty saying no. If I didn't live in this town, I wouldn't feel guilty."

"Since you are so visible in the town, how can you distinguish between what is connected to your work and what isn't?"

"It was easier to get—lost—when I lived in Camden, not be so visible. There, I wasn't so much 'Mike the Postmaster.' Here, I'm more aware of myself, and my conduct. That's because it's *home*."

"How do you change your conduct here, in this town?"

"Professionally, there are expectations. I heard a basketball player talking about his professional life, and I could relate to it. He said that on the court he did his job at a certain level, but off the court, don't expect all sorts of things from him, because he's not a living role model."

"So you do your job as a professional, and outside of that, you do whatever you want?"

"No, don't get me wrong. I don't have that guy's attitude, even though he has the right to be the way he wants to be. But it's different in this town. For instance, I'm not the most patient driver. If I'm driving in another town, my reaction to being cut off or something might be different than in this town. In Union, I'll let things slide. I really need to be mature in Union, because tomorrow, I might see that same person across the counter."

"So your work life and your commitment to the community have something in common and similarly affect your behavior," I said.

"I accept the standards of conduct, but I don't accept that I have to participate in everything presented to me. Maybe that's because I have two young kids, and I only have so much energy. By the time they're teenagers, maybe I'll feel different. Maybe not.

"Is there something special about the people here?"

"There's a difference between towns. For instance, the Barrows family—when their house burned—look at the outpouring. They had been here not any time at all, and I said to myself, this is really cool. There's a lot of nice people in this town." [Those unfortunate enough to suffer from something like a home fire are offered support by the townspeople in the sponsoring of a benefit meal, which will be attended by friends from within the community that the recipients never knew they had.]

"What is it about any particular town?" I asked.

"In Camden," he replied, "it's the ocean and the shops—that's what Camden is, but I'm not an ocean person, and I don't do shops—that's just not me. I'm a lake person. My mother has a camp in Belgrade, and we go out there during the summer. The town's like a mirror image of Union, and I'm on a lake. It's perfect for me. Here in Union, there's the Common, and closeness, a feeling that everybody knows everybody, but still, nobody's bothering you."

"You mean the people in town leave you alone?"

"That's not exactly it. For instance, all my neighbors are just the greatest. Anything they can do, they're there, and it works both ways and it's genuine; but our lives aren't really mixed, and we respect each other's space. The funny thing is that they always seem to know what's going on. It's a quiet sense of caring."

"Was it like that when you lived in Augusta?" [Maine's capital, Augusta, has about 20,000 people]

"In Augusta, you knew the people on a couple, three streets and whatever else, like if you had an outer circle in sports, but that would pretty much be it."

"Whenever I return to Union from a trip," I said, "as soon as I cross the Union line, all of a sudden I feel safe, that if anything happens, this is the best place to be."

"I agree," he said. "You never feel like you have to lock your door or worry about your kids. The pace is slower, and there isn't the feeling that you have to keep up with the Jones. Nobody's going to lay anything on you."

"Yet you didn't feel that in Augusta. Do you think size has anything to do with those feelings, or can cities be divided up into units that feel like community?"

He leaned toward me. "New people move into a community, and they have needs and wants. The families already here for a long time—they're nervous about the potential changes. They don't want to lose the sense of community. Do you feel that way?" he asked me.

"I come from southern California," I replied. "It's a megalopolis there, difficult to tell one community from another. It's helpful, I feel, if we hang onto our indigenous industry in Union, especially farming, to fend off turning this place into a bedroom community. Farms have smells, flies."

Mike nodded. "People come here from other states," he said, "and they say they don't want change, but they still want the comforts. They might come into the office and ask what to do with their trash. Well, I tell them, we go to the dump every Saturday. If not that, then they can call Dwinal. They sort of look at me. Sometimes, I'll forget, too: This is a small town. Even in Augusta, there was trash pick up. Newcomers think it's something 'abnormal' about our town, and in some town's they'll get on the board of selectmen, because they want change. Why don't they just enjoy it and become part of it?"

"At the post office, you're right on the front lines to see newcomers," I said.

"Behind the counter, we all look at each other. Nothing's said. We just chuckle."

"I well remember my first year in Maine," I said. "I was a real dude, and I almost went back to California after that year."

"How long have you been here?" Mike asked me.

"Only thirty-two years," I replied.

"I was thinking—being in the town that you work in—I thought about Bonnie [Packard]. She's been at the post office for twenty-eight years. She was born here. Her father, Basil, was a rural carrier. I consider myself friendly, but I don't compare with her. She has so much more, having grown up in this town. I feel like I belong, but not in the same…"

"…league?" I suggested.

"League—the major leagues. She's in the major leagues in being part of this community compared to me."

"There's something about staying put," I said.

"There's levels of belonging here," he replied, "even with people that may have been born here. Say they move away and come back, or maybe they live here and work in Camden or Augusta, I still have more of a sense of belonging than they do, because I work here, and they don't. Bonnie had to give up opportunities just to stay here."

"If you add up the benefits of a real feeling of belonging and knowing everyone, that's a payment worth quite a lot," I said. "Could you have stayed in Augusta your whole life?"

"It's hard to stay in one place. In Maine, if you want to go up in the world, you have to change location, like stepping stones. Postmasters, school principals, town managers, they all do it, and they move to bigger and bigger places."

"You can still live and exist in one place," I said. "It's not the same, as say in India, where you've got to move to the city or starve."

"But we in the U.S. can never have enough. We don't know how to be satisfied, don't know how good we have it," said Mike, exhaling.

"How does someone gauge his success after working twenty years at the casket factory?" I asked. "There are different ways to view success."

"It's the mindset we get from TV and movies. People need to be content to do what they want to do, and be happy with what they have, not to be concerned about what others think. When you start getting what you want, you start to forget your goals, and then there's always something else to go after. Hindsight. When I was going through it, I didn't think about it."

"Was all that sacrifice worthwhile?" I asked.

"That's a good question. From a family standpoint—maybe not the right thing to do, because I lost time with my kids, even though they've done well, and that's comfort. It definitely hurt that [first] marriage—it was a factor—how much I don't know. There's guilt there. I can tell myself different, but I still feel it, even though I really don't regret any of it."

"Is there another way to do it?"

"Sure, in hindsight. Set goals, get them, then stop. So many people are not satisfied—going on to please someone else or their own egos, and not looking at what it's doing to the family. Set goals, then stop. It's okay."

"How did you make the decision to both live and work in Union?"

"I worked ten years in Camden, and about halfway through I felt that I needed to be closer to Amy and Jac [Mike's two children from his previous marriage], and Union was between Camden and Augusta. Besides, we loved Union. I was working five or six days a week in Camden, and we [Jennifer, his current wife, and he] had plans for a family, and I couldn't see working like that—with a family. I had passed up the opportunity to apply for the job in Union years before, but my priorities had changed. Now it was family. Before, I was toying with staying in Camden for fifteen more years, then retiring, or going for a larger town and more money [Union is smaller than Camden]."

"Did you consider your decision for a long time and weigh the advantages and disadvantages?"

"Someone came into the post office in Camden and was telling me about the opening in Union. Before he finished telling me about it, I knew that was what I wanted."

"Are you a success? I asked.

"I am now," he replied, "in my own head, at least—and that's what's important."

◆   ◆   ◆

I don't want to say that Bonnie Packard, the woman Mike referred to as being in the major leagues in belonging, is a fixture at the post office, because that connotes something inanimate. She is definitely part of the post office and part of the community, as you will see. In her mid-fifties, Bonnie has a healthy glow and a ready smile. She is a continuing blonde, as are so many people these days, and her enthusiasm surfaces readily at any time.

Bonnie was born and grew up in this area and attended the Union schools through high school. After graduation, she left home to attend the University of Maine in Orono. There, she met her husband-to-be, Jim, a senior at the University at that time, but only an acquaintance when he attended the Union School three years before. Bonnie wanted to be an English teacher. However, she left the university after her first year to marry and begin a renewed life in Union with Jim, who then had a job with Bonnie's uncle, the new owner of the John Deere outlet in Union. Soon, the couple had a child, and five years later, another. Bonnie stayed at home, but within a few years, she began working at the post office part-time, and then later, full-time. I asked her how she came to be working at the post office.

"Dad worked at the post office for forty years, and they all knew me. One day I walked in to get the mail, and Walter Rich [the postmaster at the time] asked me if I had a four-wheel drive vehicle, and I said I did; and then he wondered if I wanted to go to work.

"Of course, I had to take a test, but I got a good score. I remember that there were several men from this town who also took that test, and they didn't do as well, and I got the job. They were angry that I, a woman, should get the job over them. That was the early seventies, and things were different then."

"Do they still resent you for it?"

"No, I don't think so. They're probably glad they didn't get the job. It's a hard job."

"What is it like, being from this town and working in the post office?" [Bonnie works with the public from behind the counter.]

"I know everyone's relationships to each other. My children would have gone to school with their children. They know my parents and grandparents. It makes for a huge network, and people tend to tell me things. It's amazing the sorts of things people tell me, and I get upset when I learn about bad things happening, like a death in a family. I can't be detached."

"You must be a great resource to Mike?"

She colored slightly. "Hopefully so. The post office is a place of business, and he makes the more business side of me come out. He understands that there's a lot of chatter that goes on, too, but it has to be, to keep the small town flavor. He's gotten to know many of the people that I know—who's connected to whom. It's part of our job here, what we do. I might say to him that so and so is having a hard time, and the next thing I would hear is him saying something comforting to the person. We work off each other."

"What is it like to stay put in the same town nearly your whole life?"

"It's not difficult. Camden [post office] borrowed me, and I worked there quite a while. The children were young, and I made more money. But the money wasn't a priority for me. I wanted to be available for the children. My mother didn't work, but Jim's did. It's the big question today."

"How do you view your success in life?"

She thought for a few moments. I thought I detected a bit of sadness. "I'm comfortable," she replied. "I find the job rewarding because of the personal nature of it. I enjoy the people."

"Have you ever regretted staying in Union?"

She shook her head.

"When you need to make important decisions in your life, how do you make them?"

"I go with my emotions and my impulses, not with a lot of rational thinking. Jim is very rational, and after thirty-eight years of marriage, we combine our resources to make a decision, but as in most marriages, it hasn't always been that way. I see the human-comedic side, but I need to look at the common sense, rational side, too. I would be more emotional about the decision."

"Do you look for direction for decisions from religion or philosophy?"

"Even though I'm impulsive…" She sighed. "I got my foundations from my parents and some principles that I developed myself, but mostly from my parents and grandparents, none particularly from religion. It's morals, standards in the community. I was lucky to have wonderful role models all around."

"Mike says that you have a feeling of 'belonging' here. What is it like to have that feeling?"

"It's a comfort zone. I'm comfortable with my surroundings, at least in any situation—at the store, or Hannibal's, or the Cricket. It's a relaxed feeling that I'm surrounded by things and people I know. I'm interested in seeing new things, but I feel that I do belong here. I have a step-granddaughter. We went into the market and she said, 'Nannie, you know everyone.' Some of that comes from my job and part from my living here, but I cannot imagine going into the store and not knowing someone. Traveling is nice, too, but it's good to get home."

"Have you ever seen someone from away who was able to achieve that sense of belonging?"

"Maybe not to the extent I do. You have to be second generation—seventy years, they say—to be one of us [Mainers], to have the network. Any day, I will see three or four people I went to high school with. Not long ago we got a new person in the post office and Mike warned her not to say anything about anyone, because 'Bonnie is related to everyone.'" She smiled proudly.

"Have you ever been involved with local politics, held any offices?"

"I'm more interested in national politics. I've done lots of civic things for the town, though. My dad was very active on the school board, and he was a select-man. As a child, I resented it—the time he spent away from us, even though I was proud of his contributions. It's just the way I felt."

"You and Mike are sometimes the first people in the town to talk with new-comers and the last ones to see them, if they leave. Can you pretty much tell if a person is going to last?"

"No, I'm frequently surprised. I met one girl who I thought was going to really like it here, and she ended up marrying my son."

"Do your two children live in the area?"

"Yes, both of them. I told them that they are not allowed to move any more than fifty miles from Union." She laughed.

"Do you have any regrets about your life?"

"I wish I had gone back to school."

"Why? What difference would it make to your life?"

"I enjoy learning. I was a good student, and I believe in education for education's sake—not for the diploma, just for doing it."

"What if your mother called you aside when you were a freshman at Orono, and she told you that someday you would regret not getting your teaching credential, and that you should go on to graduate?"

"I wouldn't have listened. I would still have done what I did. My daughter would not listen to me, either. I did what I wanted to do."

"What was on your mind or in your heart that motivated you to make that decision to leave?"

"We were in love, and I wanted the sort of family my parents had. I wasn't thinking clearly."

"But you were, if what you wanted was a family?"

"Not in the sense of work and education, to get a decent job," she replied. "In some ways I was mature. In others, I wasn't, and my parents were not the type to interfere. They would counsel, but not interfere."

"You say 'decent job.' Your job now seems pretty decent; to me, anyway."

"The job came along, and I got it with flying colors, and I didn't need more education. It was something that I could do, something I already knew about. It was a great job for this area."

"You knew that by quitting school you would be heading back to family and home."

"My comfort zone," she said.

"Were you homesick at school?"

"Very, but I loved it at school—the social life, everything. I was homesick, but by the end of the year, it was wearing off. It is just that in retrospect I wish that I had thought more clearly about it all. I might have made the same decision, but I should have given it more thought. I was lucky it turned out so well. It could have been disastrous."

"So the way that you make decisions—on impulse and through emotions—has not changed over the years, because you have found that way of making decisions has been successful for you?"

"Sometimes yes, sometimes no," she said, her face blotchy red.

"This was in the sixties," I said, "a time of great social change, what with the hippies, the war and all. How did it affect you in Orono?"

"I was valedictorian of my [high school] class, then at Orono, a sorority girl. I wore sweaters and skirts. The hippie thing was *not* me. I've always felt residual guilt since I don't remember feeling anything, or getting upset, about the Vietnam War. Now I would, about something like that. I think I didn't know what was going on. Nevertheless, I definitely was not a flower child. My brother was."

"Where is he now?"

"He's a professor of psychology at USM. He has authored books, done research. I try to read what he's written, but I can't get through it. Neither can my parents. He's brilliant. He has tenure."

"Are you two close?"

"We used to be close, but not anymore. Our lifestyles are so different, different worlds. He's no longer married, no children. I miss the rapport we used to have. He visits on all the holidays, but he's not interested in the children. He's just not a family man."

"So your own family came along rapidly, and since then you have applied your energies to making a good life in this town. In that way you are successful."

"I feel so. My family does."

"So you have tenure. Congratulations."

"Thank you."

We both had tears in our eyes.

◆   ◆   ◆

When I first came to Maine, I rented an apartment and made friends with a man who was originally from out of state and who worked in the construction profession. He and his wife thought that they could do well by buying houses, living in them and fixing them up, and then making a profit by selling them, moving upscale each time. That sounded good, except moving has costs, no matter how it is figured, and with each move the community changes, and there's never enough time to establish oneself in the community. Added to that, such a plan always involves one's own nest, and buying and trading one's nest is disconcerting to say the least. There is always a bigger, nicer house, or a bigger boat, whatever, and unless a person has great discipline, the chase never ends. The couple's scheme ended in a flop due to a problem they did not foresee: the dishonesty of an associate. They ended up moving to Florida.

There is much to be said about staying put, and I think Mike and Bonnie have expressed much of it. I would like to describe what I call "truth outposts," and what they have to do with staying put in a community.

Certain empathetic people within a community serve as truth outposts, and Bonnie is one of these. People tell their problems and details of their personal lives to these individuals, not because they simply want to tell others their stories, but because they want someone to know the truth as they see it, especially if rumors are flying, as rumors do. Truth outposts become especially important in a well-defined community.

My wife was a truth outpost, and, in fact, still is. People tell her the most personal things. Some knew she would relay the information to me, thereby keeping me informed on what was going on as the town doctor. An empathetic individual, people still tell Dianne their problems, even though I am no longer practicing in town, and she remains a truth outpost, just as Bonnie has been. The teller wants the assurance that someone in the community knows the truth. Someone like Dianne or Bonnie is trusted either to remain mum about what she has been told, or to let out just enough correct information to be of benefit to the situation, or act in such a way as to reaffirm the information given—without saying anything to anyone. A lot of responsibility goes along with being a truth outpost, and not everyone wants that responsibility or has the discipline to process and store the information.

In my previous book, *Personality and the Soul: Sixteen Women Show Us the Connection*, I showed how women serve as the informal system in a community to put forward many foundational qualities that I termed "soul qualities." Women serve as the matrix for the community. My wife was one of the women in that book, as was Jennifer Arbour, Mike's wife.

Most men are not as conversational and as open as women about such soul qualities. However, if a man wants to live and work in a publicly noticeable job in a community, and the man has many technical and business aspects to attend to, then he needs a truth outpost—someone who has her hand on the pulse of the community. Bonnie serves that function for Mike at work. At home, Mike's wife, Jennifer, has her own hand on the pulse of the community through her work running a nursery school within their home. Perhaps it is no wonder that Mike and Jennifer need to get away to the lake frequently. Stimulus overload can occur.

The point I would like to make here is that a man can take advantage of a truth outpost only if he stays put within a community. In a defined community, success and satisfaction may depend upon the type of input that only a truth outpost can provide.

◆   ◆   ◆

Before we leave the post office, we will speak with Buddy Savage for another angle on staying put. At the time of this interview, Buddy was out of work from the post office on disability. Rural carriers must reach across the passenger seat from the driver's seat with their right arm to stuff the mailboxes, a maneuver that results in the perfect prescription for a sore shoulder. Worse, Buddy, as tall as he is, was stuffed into a Subaru that he drove to deliver the mail.

Buddy, whose given name is Elmer, was named after his father, who died a few years ago. His mother, Christine Savage, is a Maine legislator. Buddy, his wife and two small children live in the family homestead which they now own, an old farm on Barrett Hill. We talked at their kitchen table next to an old-fashioned woodstove.

The United States Postal Service, unable to find Buddy a job within the system, encouraged him to apply for an "outside job." Buddy, approaching forty, said that he had looked into several jobs, but they all were many miles away.

"I was fourteen years at the post office in Union," he said. "I don't want to drive a long ways to work." One of Buddy's children skidded into the kitchen to check us out, then scooted out. We smiled.

"Are there difficulties in working in the same town in which you live?" I asked.

Buddy adjusted his wire-rimmed glasses on his nose. "Yeah, there is," he replied. "I generally keep to myself, though a lot of what I do puts me around people. It seems that everybody knows everything that's going on. It's a small town."

"Give me an example."

"To have somebody out there say or ask me something about my life, and I wonder how that person knows anything about what's going on, but I know that's probably the fifteenth person down the line that knew about it."

I remember some years ago someone saying that Buddy was having marital problems. I don't remember who said it, but Buddy was a visible personage, delivering the mail as he did. He subsequently divorced. No children from that marriage, and now everything seems so unrelated to that. Nevertheless, at the time, the talk was out there in the community enough for me to remember the story.

"Isn't that the way in small towns," I said. "Everyone knows your business—and your politics."

"I *know* about the politics end of it," he said.

"Your father was a town manager, and your mother a legislator. Did your father start out in politics or government?"

"Oh, no. For a lot of years he delivered bread for the Cushman Baking Company. About thirty-five years ago, the company went out of business, and he had to find another job. He had been a selectman in Union. He got a job as the town manager in Searsport [north of Union]. Later on, he became the town manager in Camden. He served one term in the legislature."

I remembered walking in Augusta a few years after I arrived in Maine and noticing a rundown car with legislative plates parked at the curb. The driver was taking her laundry into a Laundromat, which impressed me. The Maine State Library is next to the State House in Augusta, and I have opportunity to see what kinds of cars are parked in the legislator parking area when I visit the library. Over the years, the cars have up-graded some, but still they remain in the moderate price range.

"Have you held office?" I asked Buddy.

"I was a selectman in Appleton."

"With Gary Sukeforth?" [It is a small world, around here.]

"No, after that," he replied.

"This town-oriented form of government with its direct vote is only found in New England," I said. "How do you come out of town meetings feeling nowadays—good, bad, powerless?"

"A bit disgusted," he replied. "The way I look at town government, it should support the minimum of services that's deemed reasonable. It should provide less, and it should be cheaper. I'm a minimalist when it comes to government."

"Your father was a minimalist, as I recall, and your mother is pretty conservative." Buddy nodded his head in agreement.

In the 1970s, politics was more exciting and rancorous in Union. That was before the town had a manager (in addition to the selectmen) to moderate things a bit. I remember Buddy's father, so angry with me for vehemently opposing a proposal of one of the selectmen (selectwomen, in this case) that he challenged me to a fight during a town meeting. He was a generation older than I was and heartfelt when it came to politics. Had this been in Thomas Jefferson's time, it would have been a challenge to a duel. I turned him down on his offer, and years later, we nearly came to terms over other issues.

"But do you feel adrift at town meetings, that you have no power to change things?"

"I never seem to get my own way, but that's the way of it. You have to be bold to speak up. If you're not bold, then you might feel powerless. I've gone to town meetings for as long as I can remember. To get people to go to them, the meetings have to be more exciting than TV. You can't mind wearing your politics on your sleeve."

"What effect does the town form of government make on how people relate to each other in the town on a regular basis?"

"I've always lived in Maine, so I have nothing to compare it with," he replied. "What goes on in town meeting does change the dynamics of who has what in common with whom around town. There's lots of gossip, too. Suppose the town wants to buy a new fire truck. That's a big deal. People talk. And all the issues around the road crews—especially in the winter. People are more attached to what's going on."

"What's it like growing up in a town and having your father be the town manager?"

"Camden was just big enough, and I thought I could get away with things. For instance, I had just got my license, and I was trying out the car in the first snowfall, just to see how it handled, spinning round. Next thing I know, a police car pulls up with the chief of police and my father in it—I couldn't do much."

"What did you decide to do after high school?"

"I went to Orono [University of Maine] in agricultural mechanization" he replied. "I was originally in agricultural engineering, but I found that to get a job in that field you had to move out of state. I like it here."

"What's the attraction here?"

"The independent lifestyle. Maine is full of independent people—self-sufficient. I like cities okay, to visit, but I'll take the rural life any day."

"As a postman you are one of the first to interface with newcomers," I said.

"I see them come, and I see them go—six months later."

"Why do so many people come here, only to leave a short time later?"

"Whenever I travel, I always ponder what it would be like to live at that place. I think other people do the same. They travel here and they think they want to live here. There's a lot of places good to visit, but that doesn't mean you'd be happy *living* there. People have a mistaken image of this place, if they plan to move here and make a living. They get a rude awakening, unless they already have a million dollars."

I do what Buddy does when we travel and return. As soon as we cross the line into Union, I try to look at Union, as if for the very first time. Do I really want to live here? So far, I've always said yes. As I said earlier, as soon as I cross the line into Union, I feel that whatever might happen, it will work out. Maybe that comes from receiving the massive support of the entire town from one of our children's death, and it still abides within my wife and me.

"Now you're like one of the newcomers yourself," I said. "You have to find work, start over, but at least you have roots here."

"We have an acre-and-a-half planted as a vineyard," he replied. A slight smile appeared on his face. "We want to produce wine. We had originally thought of it more as a retirement thing, but we've moved up the plans."

"So you're going to do your own thing in town."

"Scary prospect," he replied. "We can get by without much money, but health insurance is a biggy with the family. Holly [his wife] might give it a try. We've been fortunate. I've made decent money, and Holly and I were able to travel—before we had the kids. Now it may go the other way—toward poverty—but I think we have a chance to do okay. We like the 'back to the earth' sort of lifestyle, but I'm not going to live in a shack in the woods."

"How is your plan coming?"

"I've got to hand it to people who have the courage to start a new business. It's a lot of work. Right now, we're practicing with eighty-five gallons of juice down in the cellar. We've applied for a license, but that takes about a year. My goal is only to make a living."

"Lots of problems in marketing," I said.

"Not if we stay *small*," he replied. "More than that is a big investment. We started with blueberries [a family-owned blueberry field], but there's blueberry wine already on the market. The price of blueberries is down because of so much production. We can barely break even."

"How did so much production come about?"

"Herbicides and bees," he replied. "We might go into marketing blueberry juice to use as an additive. We'll have the juice-making equipment. At night, when I'm not sleeping, I think of these things."

"Are you going to do this all the old-fashioned way?"

"Wine making is old as the hills," he replied. "We live sort of old fashioned, and this is an old farm. We really don't want to change it, and that's a challenge. We use modern ideas to keep it."

"Can you give me an example of that?"

"For instance, our watering equipment is solar powered. Another thing is organic agriculture. That's as old as it comes, too, but it's modern, now. There's lots of challenges. We just need to innovate, open up niche markets. If I can do half of the things that I'm thinking about, we'll do okay."

"So you are using the new to preserve the old." I said.

"Exactly."

"How about a name for your creation?"

"We're thinking of Barrett Hill Winery."

Sounded good to me.

◆   ◆   ◆

Buddy bemoans the lack of anonymity that pervades a small community. Along his mail route, people knew his business. I read in the local newspaper all the district and superior court proceedings, all the divorces and all the land trans-actions. Front-page headlines reveal that five teenagers wrecked an SUV by trying to go down a steep slope in a gravel pit. We know the boys. We know the parents who, I am certain, are still fuming, yet also relieved that no one was badly injured. In small communities, either information is passed by word of mouth, or it is in the newspaper, and occasionally on the radio.

Buddy realizes that it is most difficult to get away with much in this small community—everyone knows everyone else's business. I remember a land devel-oper in town who tried his best to take advantage of people. In the beginning, since he was from this area, people gave him the benefit of the doubt. As time went on and he mistreated more and more people, it was as though he were painting himself into a corner. He had nowhere to go—except to leave the com-munity, which he did do ultimately. Now another state has to put up with him. Again, it's hardest to stay put.

Democracy has difficulty being participatory unless it is broken into small, more manageable units that have some semblance of autonomy, making for a problem that may pose the greatest challenge to us as a society. Perhaps technol-ogy will eventually have some role in solving that problem, if it can, indeed, be solved. In the meantime, we are seeing participatory democracy in Union, and we are witnessing the freedom to innovate with the use of technology. However, none of this would work without the sense of belonging that keeps people such as Buddy planted where he is and, because he is planted here, Buddy must struggle and innovate to make it work. Without the sense of belonging, there is no sense of community, and the whole system fails. Buddy would have moved to Phoenix long ago, but maybe he doesn't like lizards.

While we are out of the center of town, I will now take the opportunity to visit the casket factory, a company that has provided so much employment in Union.

9

Standing Tall

Bill Gleason owns Thurston Bros., Inc., the casket factory in Union, and though born in Union where he lived until he was thirty, he now lives in Appleton, which borders Union and shares the same Zip Code. We need to learn more about the important component of the casket factory in relation to Union, since many of the people in Union worked at this factory at one time or another.

The factory, a long box of a multi-storied building with rows of small windows, sits above the banks of Seven Tree Pond in a small settlement called "South Union," which falls under the Town of Union. I visited the casket factory for this interview on a sunny autumn morning. Having been there several times before, I remembered the rumble of machinery. Now it was quiet. In an office looking like something out of an old photograph, Bill sat alone.

"Not much going on now," he said, turning from his desk. Trim, neatly dressed and appearing spry for his seventy-seven years, Bill had survived two heart attacks and heart surgery. I sat down and gathered my materials.

"How long have you been in the casket business?" I asked. Bill looked at me as if wondering why I didn't already know that answer.

"In 1954, Grandfather wanted to buy out the other half of the factory from the four sisters. He asked me to come in and help run the place."

"Did your grandfather help start the business?"

"No, it was his father's two brothers, Joseph and Irville Thurston, back in 1875. They used to have a shovel and ax handle mill. Then for some reason they wanted to build boxes. [I noticed that Bill rarely used the word "casket."] One brother handled the machinery, and the other the paperwork and the customers. One of the brothers had four daughters. They ended up owning half of it."

I finally knew how a man named Gleason owned a company named Thurston Brothers. "Did you want to go into the casket business?"

"I had worked there during the summers, but right then I was working at a garage in town. I had been to college at Orono after World War II. I wanted to be a teacher—history and government—and I wanted to teach phys ed."

"Going back to 1954, how did you see your future when you started working here?"

"My grandfather had been working at the factory for years. I couldn't change him much, and I had to do pretty much what he said. In the 1960s, I felt we *weren't* keeping up with the times, and I told him that I could see that I wasn't heading in a good direction. Then he started to give me a little leeway—a little."

"So what did you do?"

"If I went into the mill and I saw something that needed changing, I would get agreement to change it. Then, later, one of the older workers would come into my grandfather's office and complain about it, and that would be it. He wouldn't make the change."

"What did you do then?"

"I got pretty discouraged, but then my grandfather began to be sickly. My brother Dick and I decided to pay off the mortgage to the sisters and run the business—bring it up to date."

"Would you have been able to accomplish something more important as a teacher that you couldn't accomplish here?"

"I did my job here. I worked nearly around the clock, and I liked young people. I was a flag waver, a believer in our country, having come through the war. I wanted to instill those values in the young. I liked history."

"How does an experience in the military make a man feel that way?"

"In 1944, I was in a field artillery unit in Europe," he replied as his eyes misted. He took off his glasses. "I guess you find that life's pretty fragile—you know you're killing people. We were in the middle of the action. I did see a few of the structures we hit. There were women and children in some of them."

"So you must make a decision to support the values of this country to the degree that it's worth doing these sorts of things to protect those values? Is that how these values become cemented?"

"Yes," he nodded, sadly. "Our country is worth fighting for. At least we had support." He looked at me. "You fellows in Vietnam didn't have that support." He wiped the corner of his eye with a handkerchief.

"Were you able to instill these values, so important to you, with the people at the factory?"

"I was told that I didn't *know* anything—especially, that I didn't know anything about casket making. The crew here was very old. But I put myself through the ranks, and I learned every job—so did my brother. I was honest with the young workers that we hired. I told them that they should leave if they could better themselves—have a career with pension, benefits."

"Your customers are funeral directors, isn't that true?"

He sighed. "I had a call—just before you came in—from a man that I had dealings with for forty-two years. He was my friend, and a good customer. His business was just bought out, and they retired him. They won't buy from me now. That really upset me."

"Why is this happening?"

"I can't explain how these companies operate. It's different today. I built my business on trust and service. The truth is that two big companies drove us out of business. We had a niche for years—mostly cloth-covered units—but they wanted that niche, and it took them only a few years to take it away. These are large multi-national companies that control all aspects of the business."

"I see in your work an element of, I guess egalitarianism is one word for it, where you bring a good product to market at a fair price."

"Funeral directors are a...'special' lot," he said, being careful with his words. "Don't get me wrong, I have a good many friends in that business, but I can't explain *why* they do what they do. Many times over the years, I felt like...like I was being criticized. You see, I don't believe in expensive funerals. If you want to do something for somebody, do it while they're living. I believe in—like they say—'lower end' funerals, not the ones over $5,000. It's all over by that time."

"Why do people want to spend that much money?"

"Guilt feelings mostly—that they have to buy something expensive—and it's the last thing they can do for the deceased." Then he leaned toward me, and in a quieter voice he said, "And if father, or whomever, knew about *all* the money that was spent, he would turn over in his grave." He shook his head. "Big companies—big money—and big promotion. Because of guilt, people go into debt just to pay for a funeral. I can pick out the people that are going to spend the big money—out of guilt. I can pick them out beforehand. Just an ordinary casket is fine."

I couldn't help thinking that Thurston Brothers' caskets were neither "ordinary" nor just "fine." I well remember twelve years ago when we lost our one-year-old daughter to a tragic accident. Bill's company supplied a hand-tooled pine casket, beautifully sanded and rounded, for such a small amount. We have always been grateful for that. Five years ago, we had the same experience when my mother died.

Last year, my wife's mother died. All it took was a phone call to Bill, and we had a fine cloth-covered casket. On the afternoon of her mother's death, Dianne, my wife, was having lunch with her sister at Moody's Diner in Waldoboro, talking about their mom, her death and the upcoming funeral. When Dianne went to the cashier, she saw Bill sitting talking with a man at the lunch counter and she asked Bill if he delivered the casket to Strong's (funeral home).

He said, "Yes, everything's all set." And it was. In fact, he was on his way home from having delivered the casket. We see the qualities that went into making Bill's company such a part of Union and Maine for so long. Words like "service" and "practicality" come to mind.

"I bet I can count on both hands the people that have actually come into this place on their own," Bill said, speaking of his factory. "A lot of people from this town won't even come to the door."

"Why is that?"

"Scared of death, I guess." We both chuckled. He said, "We used my brother or an employee as a model to see the fit. Or we'd have the units lined up and my sister would crawl into one for fit. You know, there was a lot of shipping in those days, and we didn't want the bodies to rub anywhere—do a lot of damage, it would. People couldn't understand that. Made them shudder."

"So how did the business survive?"

"The checkbook started going down, and we had twenty-four people working for us, and we were putting out less than forty units a week. Back then, if you hired a person, you hired him for one job, for instance, just for moldings. The molding man would plan his day to finish the work he needed to do. We had to have production to stay alive and still maintain quality." He tightened his lips. "I lost some good friends. They needed to be able to do more than one job, but they didn't want to do that, and we had to let them go. Some of them never spoke to me again up to the day they died. But production did increase and we were putting out one hundred units a week with just fourteen men, and we maintained our quality."

"How would you do things differently, if you had it to do over again?"

"The thing I regret the most..." He paused and swallowed. "My wife—one heck of a woman. She worked, never complained, dinner was always ready—whether it was nine or eleven o'clock at night. We're married fifty-two years, and I regret that we didn't do more together. I can tell you, if I had a woman that didn't agree with me, I would have had big trouble."

"I'm trying to come up with one word that describes the quality that you express in your work," I said. "Dedication seems close, but more than that, you have been true to yourself and your value system."

"The result has been devastating," he replied, grimly. "I'm the only one here. When my son was working here, he used to make things that helped a lot, but he had to find a new career. It hurt me deeply."

I know Bill's son, Craig, who is now a well-trained nurse and paramedic. When I was looking for Bill in the factory several days later to take photos, I was surprised to come upon a couch and kitchen table—complete with a fruit bowl—domesticity within the wide open spaces of the second floor of the factory where I had seen, years before, materials lined up for a casket assembly line. Craig and his future wife lived there now.

"How is this going to turn out?" I asked Bill.

"No way I can pull this out now. The large companies have taken everything. They supply the directors with completely stocked showrooms. The homes now have coffee areas, family rooms. That all costs, even though they have," he looked up to eye me, "'considerable' markup on the units. The large companies are shrewd—they have smart people working for them—but I can tell you: They're finding it not so easy in these small towns. I see them beginning to sell off some of the homes."

"Are you doing anything now?"

"We still do small special orders, and we continue to deliver, like we always did. We're the only ones that can supply a cloth-covered pine unit."

"How about particle board?" I asked.

"Ever try to lift one of them?" he asked, looking at me. "I can pick our units right up, but even our pine units are heavier than the cardboard."

"Cardboard caskets?"

"They use 'em in place of our pine units." He said as he looked up. "Watch out for the rain." He laughed as he shook his head. "I'd like to say that there was a place for our work, but it's slowly dying out."

"What's dying out?"

"People are changing so. Now people want cremation. I can remember when there wasn't more than one cremation in ten years. Now it's an everyday occurrence. Even with our pine units, Canadians are underselling us. I can buy a Canadian unit and resell it, and still make more than on one of our own."

"Do you have plans?"

"Someone wanted to buy the place," he said as he swayed his head in a westerly direction, knowing that I would understand to whom he was referring. "He wanted to turn it into ten apartments. I wouldn't sell." He scratched his head. "Right now, it's hard with maintenance, taxes and insurance. I would hate to see it go."

I felt the same way. Everyday I could look across Seven Tree Pond and see the casket factory on the other shore—the long box with rows of windows staring out.

◆   ◆   ◆

I learned that Craig, Bill's son, was holding several jobs as an emergency room nurse and a paramedic both at a local hospital and with an ambulance service, working more than seventy-five hours a week. I remember him up until five years ago professionally racing dragsters and practicing parachuting when he had the time. I met Craig outside the casket factory as we had each pulled into the lot at the same time. Now Craig was wearing a paramedic blue shirt with patches on the arms for work. I saw that my car pretty much looked like his: an elderly, winter-beaten, Olds Cutlass. As we walked toward the factory, I noted that more paint had peeled off the building since my initial interview with Bill two years before.

Craig and I entered the factory, still quiet. His father was watching the 9/11 investigative committee hearings in his office; both he and the office looked much the same as they did when I last interviewed him. Bill said that he was still delivering special orders, that a few directors still ordered his product.

Craig and I climbed the worn wooden stairway to the second floor of the factory and into his digs—lots of wide open space, now with a pool table, plus the other accoutrements of an apartment, all partially partitioned off because of the high warehouse ceiling. We sat in the dining room. Gail, now his wife, lay on the couch in her pajamas in the living room listening to a Spanish broadcast of some sort. I knew that she worked as a night nurse in the emergency room of the local hospital.

Craig looks like his dad, stretched wider in two dimensions, but not the third. Now with gray strands in his dark hair, he moves a bit slower than what I remembered him as a young man, though some of that may be from the many hours he works now. Yet, he moves with athletic ease, much as his father still does, though arthritis will catch Bill. Quiet by nature, Craig has a laconic way of responding, but when he gets going, he is articulate and exact.

I asked Craig how he got into the nursing/paramedic business.

"At Orono, I was going to be a teacher. But I didn't continue with that, and later I belonged to the ambulance crew in Union. Then when my son [John] had the accident, I felt myself slipping deeper into it with the two months I spent down there [Maine Medical Center in Portland] with John. I was a lot readier, after that, to take the next step, which was nursing school."

While still in high school, John had been given an older Mustang convertible that Bill had held in the family—a grandfather's gift to his beloved grandson. On one of the roads below the factory, on a slippery night, John overturned the car and incurred a head injury. In a deep coma, it was thought he might never recover. I went to Portland a couple of times to meet with the family and the team of doctors and care givers. I couldn't imagine the pain everyone was going through, especially Bill. Finally, John began to awaken and, little by little, he improved. He missed a lot of school, but he eventually graduated, and now he delivers for his grandfather's company.

I asked Craig if he worked at the factory while he was growing up.

"I started when I was about eleven, doing odds and ends, but I didn't touch a saw until I was fourteen or fifteen."

"Was there pressure for you to work here?"

"Except from my father, there was an assumption by most people that I would work here. I think Dad knew this wasn't that great, but we were plenty busy. I never felt pressure. It was just a family connection."

"Your father spoke of resistance to modernization in the organization."

"People were definitely entrenched, some with up to forty years on the crew. They wanted to go in one direction: the direction they were hired on. The crew chiefs were the most resistant. Some adapted, but others didn't. They would say they would do it the new way, but actually still do it the old way."

"As you got older, you were working here more and more. Did you feel yourself being 'middled' as the boss's son?"

"More like a bridge. I could mediate the issues and say why, because I was working with the men. I could give my own opinion, and I could give feedback."

"This place has always emphasized the lower-end caskets, affordable units. Did you observe criticism of your father because he didn't believe in expensive funerals?"

"I think his heart was always in what this place did, to have a 'standard' funeral service, using low-priced wood and cloth-covered units, but hand-built by the workers. He created a little friend in mass production, but he never left the original idea. In the 1970s, he started warehousing higher-end units and would distribute them, but that wasn't his forte. He wanted to concentrate more on increased production and keep the price down on the same product."

"Was the general public afraid of this place?"

"Anyone's first time through the front door was with a lot of apprehension—friend or passerby—especially passersby. You tell them what this place is, and they say, 'Oh,' and the next thing they turn around and head over the hill."

"When your father returned from the war, he was interested in instilling values that he thought were important in young people. He studied to become a coach in college. Did you see him try to affect young people?"

"I don't know if you know it, but he was an outstanding basketball player. He played many fewer years than he should have. And he was an outstanding coach."

"Where did he coach?"

"High school, while still working here. When he coached, he put forth those values. Two or three years ago, there was a funeral service for one of the folks that played for him back then. At the funeral were fifteen or twenty people that had played for him, now all in their late 50s. Every one of them still called him 'Coach.'"

"Did he ever have an opinion about you going into the service?"

"When I finished my first year in college, I was debating whether or not to enlist. That was during Vietnam. By that time, Dad had formed an opinion about the war. He had talked to some of his ball players about the war, and when asked, he would advise them to take a good account of it before they went that way. He was too 'old school' to ever encourage anyone to go to Canada, but he might encourage them to stay in school.

"As justified as he felt about the war that he fought in, and regardless how anyone feels about war, I'll always remember what he said to me—that war was still nothing but legalized murder. And when some of his boys from the team came back from the war—those that weren't in a box—he started to talk with them about what they went through, and he really became discouraged. He said that some wars were worthy, but that one was not."

"Your father is a man of values, but in some ways, his application of his value system to his business was a significant factor in his business falling off."

"He didn't change with the industry, which went very upscale, with huge moves to merchandising, advertising. He didn't keep pace with what the funeral directors found themselves heading for at the time."

"Do you think he kept heading in the direction that he did because of inertia or was it a matter of courage, of belief?"

Craig exhaled and thought for a moment. "I think he might have wanted to make a better adaptation than he did, but I don't think he would ever have changed his mind on what was right, that the low-cost funeral is the right thing. Mostly, he wanted a way to do it."

"Did he look to you for a solution to his conundrum?"

"If he did, I was not aware of it. We talked about it and tried to come up with ways. We were years behind the power curve to begin with. Our direction was so embedded that we couldn't reverse it, and we had lost our client base—going from 130 to just fifteen clients in no time at all. It boiled down to the fact that choice was taken away from him. The directors by that time were locked into clever merchandising programs by two very large companies that blocked us out. Even the casket manufacturing organization, which we had been charter members of since 1913, went from 600 members to about eighty, with the key offices being filled by the large players."

"Did you feel that this business was a creative outlet for you, that you could put your ideas to work here?"

"I wasn't involved in direct operations until I was in my thirties, and then I was mostly doing trucking. I had my own trucking firm."

"I get the image of your father refusing to compromise with the new directions, and he would just as soon go down with the ship."

"Yes, going down as a family business. It's been in the family for 129 years. I never envisioned myself taking over the reins. I liked the people we did business with, but through manipulation of the industry, the consumer is getting hosed to buy upscale, to go into debt for a funeral. I have a hard time with that. Dad has a hard time with that."

"You have seen some difficult times here. What was the most difficult?"

"That's when my cousin committed suicide. It was an awful night to begin with, the whole building shaking with the wind off the lake. Horrendous night. We all came together. We all had tons of things to do the next day. It was emotional, stressful and I ended up having to go to Aroostook [northern Maine] the next day."

"Did his death make a difference in the business?"

"Dick [the deceased boy's father and Craig's uncle] was a real personable guy, and he liked being in the sales end. My father liked being in the back, in management. Dick was at the conventions, predictable, visiting the homes every six weeks. He was so emotionally affected by his son's death that after it all, he needed to go somewhere else, get away from this industry. If he had stayed, we probably would have been more aware of what was going on, what we could have done, maybe increased the merchandising and tried to floor entire units. A lot of the funeral directors knew my father by phone, but they didn't know who he was."

In the early 1970s, I was single and living in town, and I dated Janet, Craig's cousin's widow. Janet lived in town with her two small children. The family was still gathered over the suicide, though it had been perhaps two years since. Janet eventually married an industrious woodcutter with his own business, and they started a health club in Union, though it's now for sale. I raise this little story because of the feelings of connection I felt with Bill and Craig through these various channels.

"Do you think the funeral business is crooked or jaded in some way?" I asked Craig.

"I think the funeral directors lost their options, and they were unaware what would happen when they signed the contracts with the large company. Usually it was a five-year contract, and I don't know that many have elected to continue after that. A lot have gone out of the business altogether." Craig smiled. "But to answer your question, there can be a shady part to this business, like in all businesses."

"What do you mean?"

"We had some business with a Massachusetts firm which seemed kind of borderline. All of a sudden, that business folded. One afternoon I was out on the ice, and I looked up and saw a salmon-colored Cadillac pull into our yard followed by a truck. From the Cadillac poured men in shiny suits and shoes, all of whom seemed like the 'business men' you would see in [the movie] Goodfellas. I climbed up the hill to meet them, and they opened the back of the truck and said they wanted to sell some caskets. The truck was full of high-end units—$4,000 to $5,000 apiece. They wanted to know what I would pay. So I got my dad and he said that he didn't want any of them. They kept lowering the price, until finally they said they would sell him the entire contents of the truck, all for $600. My dad still refused. Then they said they had to leave, but they also said that they couldn't take the truck with them, and could they leave the truck and pick it up next week. My dad let them do it, and sure enough, someone showed up the next week and took the truck."

"What happened to the units?"

"They were sold to some of the local directors."

"Bill ["Wild Bill" from the trash business] worked here," I said.

Craig laughed. "He had the oddest job interview of anyone. He was out thumbing a ride, and my father picked him up. Before he got into the car, he yelled through the window, 'Bill, can I get a job?' Dad gave him a job, and he stayed a long time. I have a great picture of him holding a glue brush."

We both smiled, both holding our own pictures of (Wild) Bill in our minds.

◆   ◆   ◆

Maine practicality and tradition do not compete well in the rapidly changing industrial world where the competition believes that they must control all aspects of the business. Take a depressing Amtrak ride down the East Coast passing all the abandoned brick factories. Up until the 1920s, a standard gauge railway ran next to Bill's factory and into Union to haul out limerock and caskets. Remnants of the old roadbed running down the side of the lake can still be seen.

The two brothers had the idea for the casket-making business, and the idea worked. Bill carried on and maintained the values of trust, service and affordability. He improved upon the original idea with ideas of his own. Without the infusion of more ideas and change, the old dies, and as much as I look across the lake and believe the factory to be part of Union, I more frequently think that I am referring to the past. Yet, I have a glimmer of hope for it. Bill is still standing tall.

We can go back to our walk through the Common. Across the road from the post office, we pass by the Heath homestead, an old white clapboard Cape, and next to it, we see the two-storied business with Butler, Maxcy & Heath imprinted over the front door.

10

Pressure Release Valve

In an old storefront on the Common is Butler, Maxcy & Heath, Inc., a plumbing and heating/fuel oil and propane delivery company. John Creighton started the business, though Robert Heath, Chester Butler and Boynton Maxcy purchased it in the 1950s. In the early seventies, Robert Heath took over the business, running it until the 1980s when he retired, at which time his son, Alan, took over. Robert died in a car fire in the nineties. Alan's mother continues to live in the house next to the store.

Alan lives over the store with his wife, Genie, and two of their three children, the oldest child now independent. One daughter is enrolled at University of Maine in Farmington, and the youngest is still in high school. All three of the Heath children have Alan's build and very blond hair. Alan and I talked in the living room of his mother's home, comfortable with upholstered furniture of the 1980s. In another room, we could hear cheering as members of the family watched the New England Patriots' football game. It was Sunday afternoon.

Alan is trim and usually dressed warmly for his work. His voice always modulates a couple of steps above a whisper. He is known not to say more than is necessary.

Except for a display of old bottles placed there by Alan's mother, the store once pervaded nothing but a male touch. Spare appliance parts were littered about piled in disarray in various corners and cubbies. Within recent years, the store has been remodeled and organized, well lighted and it very much looks like an appliance business. The old bottle display is now gone.

I wanted to know if Alan had always planned to run the business after his father retired, or if he had intended to do something else.

"I considered being an architect. I went to UMA [University of Maine at Augusta], and I worked here during the summers. I finished two years of college and then decided in 1974 to do this full-time."

"Why did you give up your other plans?"

"I enjoyed working here and living on the Common."

"Now are you the sole owner?" I asked. Alan nodded. "A bunch of people have worked with you, sifted through this organization—Richard Kirkpatrick is one of them." Alan nodded again. "Some of them are doing the things that they learned working with you. Do you see that as competition?"

"No. There's plenty of work. We had considered enlarging, but we intentionally dropped out-lying fuel delivery routes, because it just wasn't feasible. I no longer do much plumbing, because I don't have the time."

"Do you have a goal in your business?"

"My only goal is to survive it."

"Does that mean it's difficult?"

"Long hours," he replied. "I used to work twelve-to fourteen-hour days. Now I try to do eight hours a day."

"Is that a problem?"

"We do just as well without the overhead of more employees. Now we have only three."

"Do you have time to do other activities, say with the children?"

"For many years, I couldn't get away, but now I make the time."

"Do you have plans?"

"We can't change course until the kids are out of school."

"Your wife helps you in your work. Before getting married, did she ever work elsewhere?"

"She studied to be an X-ray tech, then she worked for two years in Machias."

"Does working right on the Common involve you in political issues around the town?"

"We avoid that."

"Why?"

"There's enough people who have their own agendas around town."

"So they don't need your input?"

"If there's a situation that needs input, I don't hesitate. But most things don't make a difference one way or the other."

"Since you considered becoming an architect, you must have an element of creativity in you. How do you express that?"

"The job is pretty much the same. I find creativity outside of the business."

"Explain that."

"Involvement in the Masons."

"Tell me more about that."

Alan became markedly more animated. "The Masons give me a chance to net-work with people around the country with different beliefs and values. Masonry, at its core, is a study of the arts and sciences. There's lots of history involved. I find myself buying two to three books a week—lately, in history. I'm able to apply this knowledge, because freemasonry involves knowing about people and the world. I thoroughly enjoy it. It's difficult to explain without experiencing it yourself."

"Is your family involved with this, too?"

"I'm not so active in the local lodge now, but more so all over the country. We make visits to other lodges."

"And are you well received?"

"Yes, well received, and we automatically network with these people. In Maine alone there are 193 lodges."

"So with your work, your family and the Masons, is there any other important component to your life we haven't talked about?"

"Not right now, that's really enough."

"Would you change any of this if you had to do it over again?"

"Not sure I would. I'm satisfied."

"Has the character of your work changed over the years?"

"It's very different. I used to know everybody in town. If there was a problem, I knew that I could work with the person involved. Now, people don't know their neighbors, and they don't know us, and they don't care about each other. A lot of people live here, but they work elsewhere—they only sleep here. The sense of community is disappearing in many ways."

"Let's take an example," I said. "Friday night, our gas stove sputtered out while my wife was baking cookies for an event on Saturday and for the Christmas tree lighting ceremony on the Common. She said that we had run out of gas and sure enough, no gas was coming out. I told her that I would contact you in the morning.

"Saturday morning I knocked on your door. When called to the door by your son, you appeared in your bathrobe, a bit bleary-eyed, listened to my story and that was that. I left. I didn't ask if you would fix it, nor did I ask to know when you would fix it. I simply assumed that you would take care of it.

"Within an hour, you arrived and filled the tank. When you were finished, I met you in the dooryard where you informed me that the tank wasn't empty. We went inside and checked the gas range, which was then working just fine. You thought moisture had frozen in the lines, and you added dry gas and told me that you would return to change the regulator if the problem occurred again. Later in the day while my family was out, you and your wife returned, entered the house to check the range again and, apparently having finished what you had to do, left. When the family returned home, everything was fine.

"That's a long story," I said, "but how might that story go if it were somebody that you didn't know, a newcomer?"

"We're a lot more careful that the person specifically says that it's okay to go into a house with no one there—and more than that. For instance, I was called about a furnace recently, and the person said that the regulator had to be replaced. I went over, and I found that the regulator was fine—the problem was something else. Before I could do anything, though, I had to talk to them and explain *why* it wasn't the regulator and *why* I had to replace the other thing. There's a lack of trust."

"I thought that was one of the reasons a person chose to live in a small town," I said. "You can call the local repair person and know that he or she will take care of things, and you don't have to be paranoid about anything."

"That's the problem," he replied. "I know the names that go with the houses, but many of the people, I've never met. They're gone off to work when I show up. They work out of town, and the people they associate with are people they meet at work, not here in town."

"Socially, do you primarily do things with family or friends?"

"Mostly with family," he replied.

"So maybe it's people without families or extended families here in town that depend on their work relationships for social diversion?"

"If people are working in Rockland or Augusta, they don't mix in the community and meet the neighbors and talk. It's strange to me, because some days I can walk into the grocery store and not recognize any of the people. I used to know them all."

"I'm beginning to get the feeling that you and I are relics of the past. Do you feel as if you're a relic?"

"Definitely. For instance, some high school kids wanted to interview me about the Shrine and Masonry, and I thought they were interested in the public service aspects of the organizations. Turned out that they were researching subcultures. I figured the Masons were mainstream, but I guess not. Now I'm reduced to a subculture."

"Going the way of the Grange," I said. I mentioned the Grange, because I joined the Seven Tree Grange in my early days in the town. The Grange was once a farmers' cooperative, and when I was a member, I found it to be a social club with no public service activities at all, the centerpiece of the meetings being a grand lunch following the formal meeting. During the formal meeting, there was considerable parading around and some mystical sayings, but the lunch played the biggest part. The Seven Tree Grange has since been sold and an antique business replaces it.

"Why live in a small community and not be a part of it?" I asked.

"My opinion," he replied, "is that the baby boomers come from smaller families, and they're more selfish than the generation before. They live more for themselves."

"But having your mother and father born here, and your mother a Butler and her family going back to the founders of Union [more than 300 years ago], with all that background, you don't have to make a decision to be part of the community, you automatically *are* part of it."

"It's odd," he replied. "My kids want to stay here, too. I've told them that they could better optimize themselves elsewhere. Tom is working in Boston as a computer specialist, but he comes home every Thursday to go to the Masons here in town. I told him they have Masons in Boston, but that doesn't matter to him. He spends the weekends here. Jessica wants to return here as a teacher. I've told her that she won't make money as a teacher. That doesn't seem to matter to her, either."

Alan called his son, Tom, into the room to hear what he had to say about coming back to Union. I hadn't seen Tom since he was much younger. Now he was a longer and thinner version of Alan, quite friendly with a firm handshake. Alan asked Tom why he didn't just live and stay in Boston.

"I hate Boston," said Tom. "I've done the big city thing, in Boston and Rochester, and they're too fast, too many people. What I love is community theater, and I can come back here and do that. It keeps me functioning. Computers are frustrating."

"Why community theater?" I asked. "Most people go off to Boston or New York to be in professional theater."

"I can say that the best theater is here in mid-coast Maine. You find that type of community theater only here. Community theater is entirely different, of course. You don't get paid and the hours suck, but the people in it love it, and they are willing to take the time to do it. You won't find that in professional theater."

We excused Tom, because he wanted to return to the football game. Alan leaned toward me and said in a lowered voice, "When Tom wanted to go into computers I told him that networking was the field to go into. They make hundreds of thousands of dollars a year. He could have done that, but he said that he didn't like it. So I said that he should do what he wanted to do. Now he's back in *town* much of the time."

"It looks like you are an example of that yourself," I said.

"Pretty much," he replied.

"I see hope for this community if people like your son and daughter want to come back to it."

I think Alan smiled—I think.

◆   ◆   ◆

Alan has found balance in his own life through the Masons, though he feels pessimistic about where Union is heading. He sees a developing bedroom community. That's a sad commentary. I should mention what happened the night after Alan's interview for this book—one of the reasons my wife was baking the cookies.

The community had the holiday tree lighting ceremony on the Common. After a bonfire, the lights on the many small fir trees were lit, and all those in attendance walked to the Old Town Hall for hot chocolate and cookies. In one corner of the hall, people sang carols while Sybil played the piano (Sybil is divorced from Craig Gleason, Bill Gleason's son in Chapter Nine), and in other areas there were groups of people standing or sitting on the old wooden benches socializing. Most noticeable were the children walking about arm-in-arm with their friends, joking, sneaking on the stage, running outside. Someone commented on the high number of children. Indeed, there were many, and I felt glad to see that. Maybe Union has a chance after all.

From Alan Heath's place, we will walk downhill on Depot Street to the Silva's.

11

Artistic License

I last talked to Stan Silva on the corner at the post office during the Founders Day celebration on the Common during the middle of the summer. The parade had just ended, and people milled about. I walked down the hill from the post office toward Stan's 200-year-old house, just beyond the Methodist church. I was heading for the church parking lot, because our youngest son had asked if he could hang out there with the skateboarders who used the lot for their activities. I was just checking.

People in town were upset that skateboarders hung out on the church parking lot. Some raised questions concerning smoking and drugs, though no one to my knowledge had ever been caught there with drugs. In response to such concerns, the town organized a committee to examine the possibility of a skateboard park near the Thompson Community Center. A committee met, and though funds were available, an agreement on a format for the park could not be reached. People talked of it turning out to be a place for kids to deal in drugs and smoke, which were the same concerns they had with the Methodist parking lot. Interest in the committee died.

I ran into Stan coming up the hill. As we were talking, my son walked up. Hungry, he was heading for the food tables. In the course of the conversation, Stan told me that he, too, was from California—Pacific Grove, which he at one time thought was the perfect place to live. But, as in all of California, people were filing in. He had met Ann, who had traveled there from Massachusetts to explore California. She had found work near where Stan lived, they fell in love and later, the couple decided to move to Maine, away from the crowds, to have a family. That was eighteen years ago.

Sitting in their living room later, surrounded by handmade and older objects of furniture, I interviewed Stan. He looked every bit a Mainer with a checkered shirt, work pants and short, combed hair. Stan has a quiet way about him, but he talks freely.

"You were a sign painter in California. How did that happen?" I asked.

"When I got out of the Navy during Vietnam, I studied graphic design. I was making some signs on the side. I learned gold-leafing and carving and I found lots of sign work—for twenty years—around the Monterey Peninsula."

"Is that what you were doing when you met Ann?"

"At that time, I was sort of hippie-ish. I tried to grow my hair long, but I couldn't do it, and I didn't drop out. That was during the era of Haight-Ashbury. From where I was renting in Pacific Grove, I could walk to the beach. I found I could get by doing just a few signs a week. It was great. Originally, it was a Methodist church town, and the beach was all tent lots. Then beach shacks were built on the lots. Now it's all cutesy houses on those small lots with high prices, really high prices, and they name each house. You see Porsches and Ferraris parked in the driveways."

"What attracted you to here?"

"Ann's parents lived in Damariscotta [a coastal town twenty miles south of Union]. We wanted a quieter lifestyle."

"What's the advantage of a quieter lifestyle?"

"I'm a slow person. I need time to figure things out. I like to have the time to pay attention to my work." I knew what Stan met by "slow," and I also knew that he could make just about anything with his hands.

"So you came to Maine to run your sign business," I said.

"It was a great awakening for me," he replied, and then he sighed. "My first winter—and it was a cold one. My first home. Our first baby. That was in '85. We were low on money. The house was old and needed a new roof—that alone took all our reserves. I remember one day, it was minus twenty-two degrees and I couldn't keep heat in the barn. I would run back and forth between the house and barn to paint a sign."

"But you seemed as if you were doing well for years," I said.

"I'm a graphic artist, and I painted or carved signs, did the art work, gold leafing, decorative iron work, gates, even gunstocks, but this is a small town, and I had to pick up additional work from the coast. It kept us alive for twelve years, but with two kids and an old house, we got into debt, mostly through credit cards. That's the sort of debt you can't get rid of: 22 percent—Mafia rates."

"You needed money, so what did you do?"

"I had to find another job. At the same time, I had a religious awakening. For a while, I lost weight, couldn't sleep. I began working for a marine company in Camden, doing signs on boats, gold leafing, whatever they needed."

"What happened then?"

"I worked in the paint department for three years, and then I switched to the carpentry department. But there, I found I was not quite the carpenter I thought I was. No straight lines on a boat."

"Work is tight right now," I said. "Did they lay you off?"

"Yes, but I go back for various projects. Now I'm back to signs in Union, repairing antiques and building some furniture. Ann's working full-time in Rockport."

"How has your business or your approach to the business of sign painting changed now that you are going back to it?"

"It's the business angle that's changed. Before, I would spend as much time as I needed to get it just the way I wanted it. The price never changed. Now, it's what the customer wants—that's what it will be—but still a good sign, because I can do special designs and art work. For that, the customer will have to pay for the time. If he wants a cheaper sign, then he can get a vinyl sign somewhere. I have a few signs to do, but we can't live on that."

"I can't live on my writing," I said.

"That goes for any handwork," he said. "With vinyl, the signs are done by computer, and they can last about seven years if they're done the way they're supposed to be. They have machines that can carve signs, even carve granite, all by computer, perfectly spaced, whatever graphics you want, all set up, done immediately. That's changed everything."

"These same changes are occurring at the casket factory," I said, "and with the carriage factory on the Common one hundred years ago."

Stan nodded. "You know what they say: A workman works with his hands, a craftsman with his hands and head, and an artisan with his hands, head and his heart. Art is something that draws you, pleases the eye, catches attention with its dimension, size and coloring."

"It must be very different working in Union as opposed to Camden," I said.

"Whole different feel," he replied. "At the boatyard, the signs on the boats get repainted every two years. They get $60 an hour. Out here, they want signs to last forever, and at a cheap price. I still try to do my best. Not long ago, a lady came into the shop for a twelve-by-twenty sign. She told me what she wanted with letters and style. I told her it would cost $65. Her face dropped. She said that she thought it would cost about $10. I told her the paint alone would cost that."

I looked around the room. "I can see that you make do by doing things yourself."

"I've always been able to take junk and transform it into something nice. Even when I was a kid, I used to make my own toys." He pointed out several items in the living room that he had fixed up and transformed with his magic. "People throw everything away. I love to go to the dump, but you've got to enjoy fixing things," he said. "It would be nice to go into a furniture store and actually *buy* something."

"You're a throw back to the days of self-reliance of 150 years ago," I said.

"The idea of doing things myself and getting by in a small town with art just hasn't flown as we planned, but doing that is always going to be difficult, especially with teenagers, clothes and everything else. What can I say? I am what I am."

"What is it with artists?"

"I think you're born an artist," he said. "Everything you do, then, is going to have an artist's touch. I've tried selling metal sculpture, but with 40 to 50 percent going to the retailer, I couldn't afford it. I'm not a salesman. I'm an idea person."

"Ideas," I grumbled. "They can be a problem." We sat silent, glum, for a few moments.

"I remember working in California at a lumber yard," he said, "and a couple came in who wanted to buy some wood to make a wine rack. They wanted some ideas. I got an idea for one way, then another different way, then another. I kept having mental flashes, and I must have gone through five different ideas. They became overwhelmed, and they eventually left without buying anything."

"What is your process of accessing ideas?"

"It's sort of like what Beethoven did—a theme and variation. Not that I want to exalt myself into his league, but he would come up with a basic theme that he liked, then he would continue to do variations on that theme until he came up with a combination that was pleasing. I do the same when someone comes in. They usually have a seed of an idea, and I work on it with an offshoot and then an offshoot of that, and so on."

"What about the original inspiration for an idea, the basic theme? Where does that come from?"

"Where does inspiration come from? If I knew that, I would be a very wise man. I can get inspiration from looking at the color patterns on an old door, or at a blade of grass—a magazine article, even the sky. I'm a spiritualist, so I believe the soul never dies. There's another world, and only when a person dies does he know the whole story. There are certain things we can have trust in, and love is one of those things—and art is akin to love, colors, patterns—and sounds that please the eye and ear. Art is love."

◆　　　◆　　　◆

More than a year later, I interviewed Stan's wife, Ann, once again at their home. While we talked, Stan dug up the septic system, the entire back yard now a series of open trenches. It was an early spring day with sunshine streaming into their living room, and through the window, I could see Stan with a shovel. Ann and I sat on old upholstered furniture. Their sixteen-year-old daughter, Katy, sat at the computer in the next room.

Ann, twelve years younger than Stan, is well kept and figured, her brown hair attractively long. Strikingly professional in bearing, and sincere, she has experience meeting and greeting people in her sales job at a sporting goods outlet.

Originally from Massachusetts, Ann finished college in history and political science and then went to New Hampshire to work at a ski area. After one winter of that, she and a girlfriend decided to travel by car to California and see what was out there. She ended up in Carmel and took a job as an inn manager. Almost immediately, she met Stan, who was making a new sign for the inn.

I asked Ann what her first impression was of Stan.

"I thought he was a handsome, intelligent, dedicated—and a thoughtful artist," she replied. "He also liked to camp and hike, both of which I liked, too."

"So a relationship began. Where did it go from there?"

"Neither of us had plans to get married. We didn't live together, but we were a couple for four years, starting out as friends. We decided to get married in 1980."

"Why get married?"

"It made sense, and it made things—less complicated. At some point, you want to make a commitment."

"How did you get to Maine?"

"My parents were living in Damariscotta, and we wanted to live in a quieter place. Soon after we moved out here, my dad died."

"I heard about that particular winter from Stan," I said.

"It was a rough winter. First, there was lots of snow. I had taken a job as a receptionist, and I was pregnant with Tim. Stan was trying to open the sign shop, and at the same time, we had to make the house livable. The pipes froze. The roof needed replacing, and we ended up spending all our money. At first, his shop was in this room." She gestured around her. "We had diminished living space."

"How did the sign business go?"

"After twelve years, we closed it. But the writing was on the wall. For me it was a relief—terribly frustrating. It was hard work keeping it going, and I was tired of it. We both were burned out. Then Stan started working at Wayfarer Marine, and it was a whole new thing."

"At about this same time, Stan went through his religious transformation," I said. "Did you undergo a transformation at the same time?"

"I did not. We always had an open relationship, and we each had our own view of the world. I supported him, though, in his change in religion."

"It must have been stressful," I said.

"It is stressful trying to understand it; so that I might believe in it, too. After a while, I came to terms with it, in a way. In that respect, we lead parallel lives. He goes to church each Sunday. I will go with him on holidays, because I don't want him to be alone. I suppose it's hypocritical of me, but church-going does not fit into my belief system." She thought for a moment, very solemn. "But there have been *good* things, too. He reads all the time, and he's gained a great deal of knowledge, especially about history. It's interesting to talk with him. He's become charitable and not so much the self-absorbed artist."

"What about with the children?"

"The kids bring up subjects, and Stan and I may not always agree on aspects of morality. We give the kids both views." She sighed and leaned back in her comfortable chair.

"You worked at the Cricket," I said.

"For a year-and-a-half. I liked dealing with the local people, buying things for the store, changing it."

"What's it like working for Gary [Sukeforth]?"

She laughed. "He's a great guy, and I don't want to hurt his feelings, but if you're an organized person as I am..."

I nodded. "I've been in his office."

"In any case," she added, "I was invited to work at Maine Sport, and it was a predictable and organized situation there."

"Has your life here in Union worked out as you might have envisioned it when you were in California?"

"It has not been what I envisioned," she replied. "Our life here has been faster paced than I thought it was going to be, and it's much harder to make a living. Unless you have a comfortable income, life is difficult here. We thought it was going to be more relaxing, and we would have contemplative time. I thought I would be gardening, and now I don't even have time for a garden. Part of that is having children, and also working and doing the necessary renovations on the house. We have to do everything ourselves."

"What you describe is happening over much of the country," I said. "Production is up, but income is not, and hours are longer. But it also sounds as if you had the fantasy of coming to Maine to live off the land, live a rural, small town life."

She smiled thinly. "Yes, live off the land. We read *Mother Earth News*, learned about windmills, composting. Wouldn't that be cool, we thought. But we had to spend all our money just to fix the house and start a business. It just sucked up all our money. We lost the energy for those other ideas, and we haven't followed through."

"What is your part in the business now?"

"My role is the bookkeeping. Stan is not crazy about the computer, yet."

"In many ways," I said, "Stan's work heralds back to the days when craftsmen worked by hand, as compared to today when machines make products that do the job without a lot of flourish."

"The whole idea of vinyl is now moot—it doesn't even matter, because he's not emotionally attached to that business. He's gotten away from the whole idea of signs, though he still does a few. Now he is focusing on metal sculpture. Metalwork is his love. He'll always be the artist. We are trying to widen his market through the Internet, because there isn't enough market locally to make a living. If he could be in his shop making his sculpture with someone else finding a market for his work, he would be supremely happy."

"I see you have a computer in the house now."

"I brought it into the house," she replied. "Stan has always felt that the Web was dangerous for kids. His sister and brother in California are trying to get him involved in the Internet. We all think he has incredible talent, and he would have great success if people could see his work. I want him to be happy and be able to do his work and earn a decent living. But he doesn't want anything to do with sales, and right now, I can't do it. I would probably have felt guilty about that ten years ago, but not now."

"Do you two, as a couple, see yourselves heading in any direction, toward a goal?"

"I view our relationship as an adventure, not as goal seeking. We've been married twenty-four years, and how we relate is a daily adventure. I think there is a point in which both of us have to be contented. In sharing a life, if one partner is unhappy, then the other is unhappy, too. I do hope that when we're old, we'll be able to rock on the porch together."

"People say that living with any artist can be difficult."

"It's challenging, but not terribly difficult. I've always been an optimist. It's worse, I think, for the guy that does it on his own, rather than one who works for a large company. For the guy at home, in the barn, who doesn't have a lot of contact with people, it's lonely. An artist shuts out so many things to make the creative connection. Depression is difficult, too, but I'll tell you, for me, the scarier and more serious things in life involve the kids—their traumas and illnesses."

"It takes courage," I said.

"Stan has courage," she said, giving a fending-off gesture as if to say that courage did not apply to her. "If anyone has tried to pull him *off* his artistic tract, it has been me. I do feel guilty about that. After he closed the sign shop, I told him he had to get a job—not what he wanted to do. So he worked for someone else for five years, and we both found out that he has to do his art work in order for him to be happy. My role is to try to help him find a way to do it."

"Do you feel unfulfilled in any way?"

"I've always wanted to write, but I don't do it—but not because I can't. I tend to put things off for myself with the perspective, 'When the kids are grown up, I'll do it.' That is a goal for myself, and I look forward to the time when I can pursue it. I have a particular project in mind."

"Anything else you would like to say?"

She thought for a moment. "This is a bit off the subject, but about the community. It's much better living in a place where you know your neighbors and they have lived there more than a few years. It makes life a lot easier. There are great people here, and they make it a home for us and it's a constant benefit knowing that the people around us care about us. That's the big difference between here and California."

◆   ◆   ◆

The night after Stan's interview, I was sitting in my car in front of the ten-cinema complex in Rockland waiting for some of my kids when I saw Stan and Ann coming out. They walked across the parking lot, unbeknownst that I was watching, just the two of them. Even though they were not holding hands or anything physical like that, just by the look on their faces, their gestures and the way they moved—intent on talking, probably about the movie they had just seen—I could tell that they were very much in love. That made them look young, but they could have been any age.

12

The School of Dump

The town dump, or transfer station as it is referred to these days, is a pivotal institution in the community as evidenced by the number of times it appears in the interviews. There is value in talking with my neighbor, Hank Balsley, who works at the dump. Hank and his wife, Sally, live in a small house near the road, just down the hill from us. They have fixed up the house considerably, tearing out all the interior walls on the ground floor.

It's a cold November morning, and as I walk into the house, Hank jokes that he has turned the downstairs into a large hunting camp. He has shot two deer already, and later this week he will go to Pennsylvania to hunt with his younger brother. The heads of two large bucks adorn the pine walls. A woodstove in the middle of the room provides all the heat they need.

Hank looks robust and active. I've always known him to have a beard. His body is compact, and he generally wears suspenders. He has a moderate Southern accent. I asked him about working at the dump.

"I enjoy working over there. Ain't that hard of a job. Other than having to put the tarp over the garbage truck, it's a tit-job."

From where I sat at the dining room table, I could see a small photo of him in a Coast Guard chief petty officer's uniform. I mentioned his military career.

"Four years in the Navy and twenty-six in the Coast Guard—chief engineer. Retired in '85."

"How did you end up in Union?"

"Sally's from Owls Head [south of Rockland]. We got tired of paying rent, and we wanted a place that was cheap—a fixer upper. That's what we got here. I figure that all those that lived here before was poor. I've torn this house completely apart, and not once have I found a single coin. When they dropped even a penny in one of them cracks in the floor, they must have taken a knife and dug it out."

"You're from Pennsylvania originally?"

"I'll be going back there for two weeks. By the end of that time, I'll be plenty glad to get back here. Turn on the news down there and you get two hours of crime. It's a rat race, but in the fifties when I left, it wasn't like that—in Cornellsville in southwest Pennsylvania. Now it's all four-lane highways and shopping malls."

"When you moved here, I saw you doing a lot of farm work."

"I still do. I work with Vince. Mostly I do tractor work in the spring. Sometimes in the winter I'll help to fill in." [Vincent Ahlholm runs the largest farming operation in the area. He owns patches of land in several towns, one of them being adjacent to Hank's property, where Vincent grows cabbages, pumpkins or squash, depending on the market.]

"What's it like to live next to a working field?"

"It's okay, except when he had the chicken barn [just down the road] and he spread the chicken shit on the field. There were so many flies, I had to hose off the doorway just to get into the house. We bombed the house, had fly tape all over the place. Sometimes there was so many of them on the window screens, you'd think it was dark."

I remembered the time of the flies very well. We had the same problem. Flies covered the sunny side of the house. Up and down the road complaints abounded—largely about the flies coming from the chicken barn, but also about the rats. As the health officer for the Town and with so many complaints being made, I finally was called. The selectmen wanted me to inspect Vincent's chicken barn to discover any possible health hazard. I did the inspection, and Vincent wasn't any too happy with me, or with the inspection. Nobody was happy. Philosophically, I thought that farming and Union had to make accommodation to one another; still, nobody was happy. In the end, Vincent gave up the chicken business—it was an awful business, anyway—and that solved the problem. After that, my family returned to having our large Fourth of July parties at the house. We had been having them for twenty-five years, but had to stop because of the flies in the food.

"I'm interviewing you because so many people in these interviews mentioned the dump," I said.

"Something the matter there?" Hank asked, anxiously.

"No," I reassured him. "They like the dump, but the subject keeps coming up. The dump is an important part of community life."

He sighed with relief. "We just had a group up from Waldoboro thinking about copying how we do things. Only thing is, I'm glad we started pay-for-bag right at the start. Then you don't have to go through the hassle of getting it passed after you've already opened." [The townsfolk must purchase large plastic bags for household garbage, available at any store in Union, and the dump accepts pretty much anything, as long as it is in one of those bags.]

"Once you have the bags," I said, "if you need more money, you can always increase the price of the bags."

"We never have," he said quickly. "Also, we have our own truck scales. No arguing there. We weigh 'em when they're empty, and we weigh 'em when they're full. Whatever it weighs, we pay. We also try to keep it nice over there."

"In one of the buildings, I see all sorts of stuff for sale, furniture, books, appliances. How does that go?"

"That's not for sale," he said. "That's the free pile. If something comes in and it looks good, we'll put it in the free pile. People don't fix nothin' now days. They throw it away. If it's halfway decent to good, it won't stay there very long."

"That's the essence of recycling," I said.

"People drive by just to check the free pile. Sometimes a person will ask if we have something or other, and I can say that if they're looking for anything in particular, and they're not in a rush, it'll eventually show up."

"How did the free pile come about?"

"It was like that from the start."

"So there's a large element of public service in this operation," I said.

"Oh yeah," he replied. "And you know, 99.9 percent of the people that come there are super."

"What about the others. What's their gripe?"

"Having to buy the bags and put the garbage in the bags, but they get used to it, 'cause there's no other way."

"How about the recycled papers—from the offices—can people go through that material?"

"We used to allow dump picking, but not anymore—too many lawsuits. Now, when it's in the bin, it's gone. That goes for the metal or wood bins and all the recycling bins."

"Who has the responsibility for the dump?"

"The board of directors, one selectman from each of the towns."

"Do they know what's going on?"

"They all bring stuff there, and they see what's going on."

"Do they get paid anything extra for that?"

"Nope."

"Another reason I wanted to talk with you was about farming," I said. "Farming, though it's dying out in Union, still plays an important part in our lives."

"In my opinion," he said, "with the price of land and the taxes going up, the farmers can't afford to keep their land. Someone comes along and offers them a big price for the land, and pretty soon you see a house there." [Since this interview, Vincent sold the field next to Hank's, and a house now sits there, built by an out-of-state retired couple.]

"Where are the markets for the farmers?" I asked.

"You wouldn't know it, but Vince is the biggest cabbage farmer in the Northeast. He has one thousand ton of cabbage stored, and it'll all be gone by May. Most of it goes to Kentucky Fried Chicken into coleslaw. He also sells to Chinese restaurants and Morse's for sauerkraut."

For years, we've had the smell of cabbage coming from the fields in the fall. Jamaican laborers work the fields. We wave to them from the car as we pass by the fields. They wave back. Iris, our youngest daughter, always stares, since she has Jamaican heritage.

I knew that Hank recently had a serious operation for prostate cancer. I asked him if going through that caused any changes in his life.

"I do what I've always done," he replied. "I said to Sally that there ain't no time left, so let's get our lives set. So, we got everything set up. I know if I go, she'll sell the house. She wants to return to salt water. That's where she's from."

"How about your daily lives. Did you change any of that?"

"No need to change that. We both do what we want to do already."

"Do you go to town meetings?"

"Not many," he replied. "In my opinion, you go to town meetings, and they know you're an out-of-stater, and they don't listen. It's run by a few, for a few. The relations of the founders of the town—they're the ones that run it."

"Let's say that you were king and you could change things as you saw fit. What would you change?"

"That's a hard question," he replied. He thought for a few moments. "One thing—the way I feel, if a guy owns a piece of land and he's not delinquent on his taxes, and as long as he doesn't pollute the river or somebody's well, then he should be able to do what he wants with his land. If Joe Blow wants to clear-cut his land, then he can do it. Hell, in ten to twenty years, it'll be grown back. I just don't believe in interfering in other people's business. In a way, there's too much government."

"You're basically talking about having more freedom?" I asked.

"Yeah. They holler about gun laws, but there's enough laws on the books right now, that if they really enforced them and punished these guys, we wouldn't have so much crime. The judicial system doesn't work. The lawyers got smarter or somebody's got a lot dumber. Not long ago, a drunk driver killed somebody and come to find out, he had fifteen OUIs [Operating Under the Influence] before that. Why didn't they do something long ago? The criminals down in Warren [Maine State Prison]—it's the Taj Mahal. They have pool tables, TV."

"So if you were king, you would allow more property rights?"

"Yes, and I would have punishment equivalent to the crime—eye for an eye—I'm a firm believer in that."

"In your philosophy there's a large element of responsibility," I said.

"People have to take responsibility for their actions," he replied.

"How about a politically hot issue, like abortion?"

"If raped, then it's not her responsibility, but if she's living with some guy, then it's their responsibility and they need to take care of the kid, or give the kid up."

"Did your idea of responsibility come from religion?"

"My parents felt the same way. If you had a kid, then you have to get off your dead ass and support your family—not welfare—instead of laying around and making more kids. It's a responsibility. If you're not going to keep 'em right, then don't have 'em. It's like with a farmer—if he's not going to take care of the cows, why does he have 'em? Welfare's good for somebody that's disabled, but a person shouldn't get more welfare just because they're having more kids."

"You didn't say where this value of responsibility came from."

"I was brought up on a farm, big family—three sisters and four brothers. My father was a farmer and blacksmith. He never went a day without working. Had his own fighting chickens, made his own wine, grew the corn to make his own moonshine. Made us work on the farm, too. My summer vacations were spent at the end of a hoe handle."

"Was there religion?"

"My mother was religious. She never missed a Sunday at church, but she didn't beat it down our throats. My father never went to church in his life."

"Did the children go?"

"My mother insisted we go to Sunday school, but not to church, unless we wanted to."

"What effect did that have on you?"

"Sure didn't hurt me any. I don't go to church myself. I'm not religious. I believe in God, but I don't live by the Bible."

"Yet through your parents, you had models: hard work and belief in God."

"Every day we had certain things we had to do and help with. Mondays, for instance, would be washday. Ironing on Tuesdays. Some days would be field days, and we would change all the sheets and clean up. Even the boys had to do the dishes."

"Did this bring the children closer together?"

"The two older children got everything: the farm and all. They said they would stick around, but they didn't."

"You mean your parents died when you were young?"

"My mother died when I was nine, and my father died when I was fourteen."

"What happened then?"

"I had to quit school in the eighth grade and get a job so we could eat. My younger brother and I cut logs. It was lucky that we weren't sent to an orphanage. We lived in the old house, and my older sister got married and went to New Jersey. My older brother got mixed up with a woman with three kids. He brought them all to live with *us*. The four of us younger kids, we made life miserable for them. We drove them away. We figured we could live better by ourselves. That brought the four of us younger ones closer."

"When you dropped out of school, did you feel that you didn't need it, or did you feel that life was passing you by?"

"Neither. If I wanted to eat, I needed to earn money."

"How did the military fit in?"

"Later on I joined the military. So did my younger brother. I had the military to fall back on, but now you gotta have education. Back then, if you were young, or in trouble, it was thought that they could send you into the military and straighten you out. I got my GED in the military. I liked it. That's why I spent thirty years in it. I wouldn't fit in now."

"What is the reason for that?"

"Why isn't in my vocabulary. Back then, if I was asked why, all I had to say was that's the way it's got to be. No more questions. It isn't like that now."

"I see a great deal of thought in your life. It fits together." I said.

"Kids today are given too much," he replied. "They don't have to work for nothing. They want the best without doing anything to get it. I try to beat it into my grandkids' heads that education—that piece of paper—will open more doors than anything. I never had the chance, but they throw away the chance. They laugh at the bookworm, but later on, they'll be working for that bookworm. I sent my GED to the high school at home, and they sent me a diploma."

We paused in thought. "Is there anything else you would like to say?"

"I try not to stick my nose in other people's business, and I don't want them sticking their noses into mine." he replied.

"Is that 'Live and let live'?"

"Right. And I'm big on family values. Sally works a little, and what she makes she can do with what she wants. It's like my dump money. If I see something I want in a catalogue, then I get it. Between the two of us, though, everything is ours, not mine or hers."

"It's a partnership," I said.

"Very much so, and I know she feels the same way. Everything is ours, and we get by just fine."

◆   ◆   ◆

Hank has a small farming operation of his own behind his house in neat bushy rows of raspberries and blackberries. My sons help with the picking. He and Sally are kind to them, and they pay well, but the berries also sell well. Restaurants and grocery stores gobble them up. Like many Maine people, Hank and Sally have a variety of income sources, and they enjoy doing each of these activities.

Hank has had to prove himself with good results in his work life. In many of the families I see in Maine, the father may have success in business, but no education. The children feel that since daddy has done so well and done it without education, why should they waste their time with formal education.

I phoned Hank. He had just returned from two weeks in Pennsylvania. I asked him why he thought education was so important.

"I never had the chance to get an education," he replied.

"Did you experience anything in the Navy that led you to believe that education was a good thing? Sometimes the most educated people are the least able to get things done."

"I had the chance to advance, but I couldn't—trying to get stuff out of the books was hard for me. It took me twenty-five years to reach master chief. Some were making it in twenty."

"You mean they could do a better job than you?"

"No, but they could do the tests. The guys with the education could advance by passing the tests. If I had an education, then I wouldn't have had to keep pushing and pushing—I wouldn't have had to struggle so much. I could have had better money for a longer period of time. My brother has worked all his life in the woods, and now that he's retired, he gets minimum social security; and he's still going to have to work."

"You are talking of the practicality of an education."

"If you don't have a chance to get something, then you want it even more," he said. "It never hurt me to learn anything, even if I never used it." He paused for a long while. "If I had an education, I wouldn't have been in the Navy. Before my father died and I had to go to work in the woods, I would have liked to have gone into forestry, maybe at Penn. State, and then do forestry for one of those large companies. I could have worked my way up. An education can lead you anywhere you want to go in life."

When we ended our conversation, I was left with thoughts of my brothers-in-law and so many other people I know who have worked in the woods in Maine. The money seems good to a young male, and to look at my wife's father, he had learned everything he needed to know by the eighth grade to work in the woods. So he quit school. Eventually he had his own sawmill, and his three sons worked for him, quitting school as their father had. It was good work until the boys tired of it and decided to go their own ways. My wife's father closed the mill, and after owning his own gasoline service station, he went back to work in the woods, using draft horses rather than heavy equipment. He fell over dead in his dooryard at the age of sixty-seven.

◆   ◆   ◆

To be educated, or not to be educated, that is the question. I talked with Gordon Libby, a self-made man and a close friend of mine who has a trucking and logging business in a nearby town. He hauls the trash from the Union dump—the transfer station. Reaching Gordon isn't so difficult because he has pagers, cell phones, recording devices and radios to keep track of the various arms of his business. The problem is getting him to stay in one place long enough to interview him. He said he would "catch up" with me. Several days later, I was working at the house when the phone rang; it was Gordon.

"I'm down at Maritime Farms [the convenience store on Route 17 where two of my children work part-time]. I can't stop at your house because I'm in the General, and we're loaded. Come on down, and we'll talk on the way to the mill."

It was late in the afternoon, already dark, when I pulled into the parking lot of the convenience store where Gordon stood next to his truck eating Oreos and drinking coffee. He was inspecting something on his air brakes. He invited me to climb into his truck, which I learned later was built by General Motors, and he had owned it since the mid-eighties. It now had 750,000 miles on it. Behind us sat thirty tons of wood chips, bound for the sawmill in Searsmont, which used the chips for fuel to generate heat and electricity. They use some twenty loads a week. Gordon offers a wood chipping service with his logging operation, snow plowing for another town, and hauls garbage from the Union transfer station to a trash burning/electric generation facility.

Gordon is a friendly person, as one would have to be in order to learn all the things he has from talking with people over the years. I knew that Gordon had quit school during his second year in high school. We were bumping along in his truck over the road beat to death by such trucks. Just behind us loomed a sleeper unit with an unmade bed. I could smell wood chips and diesel fuel. A dim map light gave me just enough light to see what I was writing. Because of the jarring, I could barely read my unruly scrawl.

"Why did you leave school?" I asked him.

"School was in the way. I couldn't wait to get in the woods and start a business," he replied. Gordon is about ten years younger than I am. Though we nearly had to yell to hear one another, he could converse with me and still maneuver the truck over this old road, crowned the wrong way in many places, with ice patches in the shaded areas.

"Would you change your course, if you had to live it over?"

"Yes, probably, but that was where I needed to be at the time. I chose to do what I did. I made all my own decisions, but I think it's important for a young person to have someone to help direct them. I could have been on the fence, and I could have been persuaded to stay in school. No one either encouraged me or discouraged me. It did make me the person I am. If I followed the path that everyone else does—on to school—then I'd be different."

"Your children see that you're successful and respected, why would you want education?"

"It might have sent me in a different direction—maybe something like engineering. More education wouldn't have hurt me. The world could have waited a few more years for me. I'm doing okay now, but I have my health, and I have to work hard. I would be the same person, but with more education, and if I had to change jobs, or work for someone else [which he has never done], it wouldn't hurt that I graduated from high school."

"What do you think of educated people? Many people with formal education end up with little sense," I said.

"They're okay, as long as they don't learn a wrong pattern, taught them by someone who has their particular viewpoint—like, 'don't cut trees.'" He was serious, not joking.

We arrived at the mill, the truck was weighed and Gordon said it was over weight; he grinned. We maneuvered into a narrow corridor in one part of the mill, backing uphill until we jarred to a halt, brakes hissing. Gordon unhooked the trailer. Nary a soul around, but plenty of light, large pipes, the noise of machinery. A man appeared who said he had to free up the conveyor because the previous load, dumped by another contractor, wasn't chipped finely enough and twigs had bound up the mechanism. Once that was cleared, Gordon went into the control house, pushed buttons on the control panel and the entire trailer lifted to a near vertical position while large augers moved the chips away from the back of the truck, and by way of a conveyor, into the large storage shed. From there it went onto another conveyor into the huge burners that powered the generators. No one was around when Gordon gave me a tour. The machinery pretty much ran itself, if monitored and maintained properly. This was an independent business, owned by a family.

We met up with the same man—we will call him Russell. Gordon had known Russell for many years. Probably on my account he asked Russell how long he had worked for Robbins Lumber. When Russell told Gordon it had been fifteen years, Gordon asked if he would retire there.

"Retire or die," said Russell.

"You know about the second," said Gordon. They laughed.

Once Gordon had the trailer hooked up again and we were bumping homeward, I asked him how to keep employees like Russell, or his own employees, over the years.

"Everyone's different—from day one," he said. "I learned that from my own kids. To keep an employee, you have to fit their needs, and the employee has to fit mine. It doesn't always work. Anywhere along the way, something can tip the scales—like a divorce or injury. You take Russell, for instance, he's no drone. He may be simple, but he's got his own tastes—I know, because I've talked to him."

"But what qualities are important in such a person to make him a good employee? What do you look for?"

"I've got contracts to fulfill, so I need a commitment from my men. They've got to be responsible, but there's chemistry to it, too. For instance, some dogs bite and some don't, and I don't know what does that. I do know that I don't like bickering. I try not to hire that kind of person. They've got to be able to get along with the others. If there's a problem, I try to straighten it out. If I address the problem, then they come out better for it."

"You're sort of a parent," I said.

"If I don't care, then they don't care," he replied, and then he paused. "I was just thinking whether or not an employer would raise children different than an employee."

I certainly had no answer for that. I then asked Gordon if employers need responsible employees with the social skills required to get along with others, shouldn't we try to determine how to train people to develop in such a way? Then wouldn't every employer and consumer be that much happier?

Gordon glanced quickly at me as if I were crazy. "Isn't that what the Communists wanted to do?" he retorted. "You take any twenty-five kids, and you'll find all different kinds, and it's so complicated, I don't think you could determine a pattern."

I agreed with him. We were now back at the convenience store. He had to get back home for supper. So did I.

◆   ◆   ◆

Some people want to learn, some don't. Those who want to, will learn with or without school, and in their own way. What about those who don't want to learn—those who can learn, but refuse to, what happens to them? They attend the "basic" courses in school, but they rarely listen. They lead messed up lives, and eventually, if they haven't killed themselves with poor health habits, they arrive at the conclusion that they must work, and in order to work, since they are now older, they must learn something. Sometimes they can pick up the pieces, and sometimes they can't.

The high schools around here do not apply to what fishermen see as their future. Consequently, some of the fishing communities have a narrow perspective, and any change in the community meets with resistance, sometimes violence. The Maine coast can seem anything but friendly—at least to outsiders—and there is even fighting amongst their own, of the clannish type.

Some of that provincialism stems from climbing property values and taxes, brought on by well-to-do and well-intentioned newcomers who want to live by the sea. Sometimes I wonder why anyone would want to move to Maine, and I even forget all the reasons why I live here.

◆   ◆   ◆

I wanted more information about successful people who did not have much education, and I wanted to know what they thought about the potential value of education. That's a book-sized question, but I knew a person who I thought could tell me important things about the subject from her own experience. I asked Missy (not her real name) about the value of education. Missy is tall, with a thin profile and a soft voice—an all around small-town girl, with little education, but fortune has exposed her to large organizations and highly educated people.

"Years ago," she said, "I felt inferior to the educated people I was exposed to, because I only had a high school education myself. So I started to take [a few] courses. I found that I really enjoyed them. But I have learned that any security that I received from taking the courses was a false security."

"How was that security 'false'?"

"The people I am exposed to who are educated—in this case, mostly physicians—their expertise is narrow, and their education is nearly irrelevant regarding knowledge and interest in other fields, such as politics, government or art. I found that I knew as much, or more, than they did in many subjects."

"Since you no longer need the backup of education to feel secure, of what value is education?"

"If I had to go out and find a job and support a family, it would be of value," she replied.

"As an insurance policy?" I asked.

She nodded. "But I'm not a competitive person. I've found that many educated people are very competitive, and they seem to need the education for status."

I could remember my first day in medical school. Immediately, we were called "doctor." Ah, I said to myself, now I am a real doctor. As a physician, respect comes automatically, earned or not, unless the physician steps out of the field of medicine, and then he or she is just another whatever, and respect must be earned. Ego problems are occupational hazards, at least in males in the field of medicine.

"As long as you didn't need education for work," I said, "then you wouldn't need it at all?"

Being very careful with her words, she said, "Some of the most interesting people, to me, have had little education—maybe only a year or so of college." Then she laughed. "I've found it educating to be around the uneducated. Especially in big organizations—like medical centers—the people are so uptight, afraid that they might say something politically incorrect. That can be really dull."

"Had you to do it over again, would you have continued in school?"

"I can't say I would have done anything differently. I'd rather do my own thing."

I would caution anyone moving to the country not to underestimate any of the inhabitants just because they might look like "country folk." Some of the most intelligent people I know in Union don't look the part at all. I like what the novelist E.M. Forster said about education in 1927 in one of his lectures:

As long as learning is connected with earning, as long as certain jobs can only be reached through exams, so long must we take the examination system seriously. If another ladder to employment were contrived, much so-called education would disappear, and no one be a penny the stupider. (Forster, 1927)

Similar to Forster's views, I was interested that other than strictly for work considerations, formal education seemed to have little value to Missy. She, obviously, speaks as an educated person speaks. Do nearly all people go to school only so they can find a job and earn more money? That would be a sad commentary, but it gives us a clue as to why some people find school so dull.

As my son, Paul, recently told me—he's now a sophomore at the University of Maine in Orono—"If I had high school to do over again, I wouldn't have done a lot of the busy work they gave me, and I wouldn't have been concerned about grades. I would have just concentrated on things that interested me, spent time on those things, and to hell with the rest of the stuff."

Lots of opinions about education, but I do know one thing from living around here: Ignorance has little to do with education, that is, if you agree that the significant part of ignorance means to ignore. An early educational system would do well to help a child find his or her innate talents and a way to express them. Maybe with that effort, there would exist less ignoring.

Let's leave the dump and education—and dumpy education—and return to the Common, walk down the hill from the post office. We will visit the Soules.

13

Blueberry Hill

Walking from Alan Heath's store down the hill and by Stan Silva's house, then uphill to the top, we come to the cemetery overlooking Seven Tree Pond. There we find the graves of Alan Heath's mother's family, the Butlers, and the ancestors of people with names familiar throughout the town. The house just before reaching the cemetery belongs to Peter Soule.

When I first arrived in Union, a portion of Peter's house doubled as the town clerk's office, and his wife served as town clerk and tax assessor. It was a busy place during the day, with cars coming and going, people seeking marriage licenses, hunting licenses and tax bills.

Peter worked as the manager of the blueberry packing plant at the foot of the hill, where the standard gauge railway once had a depot. The street is still named Depot Street, and the present blueberry packing plant has incorporated a portion of the old depot for its office spaces. Nothing remains of the tracks, but old rail ties can be found along the way, partially buried in the forest and fields.

Peter originally lived in Portland, attended college in Orono studying agriculture and later, he studied industrial engineering for two years in Boston. He comes from five generations within the blueberry packing industry, the family business which was once headquartered in Portland, Monmouth Canning Company. They operated plants in four other Maine communities in addition to their now defunct Homemaker Baked Beans factory in Portland.

Peter arrived in Union in 1959 primed for the family business and set to run the blueberry and squash canning operation in Union, and later to oversee operations in the factory in Liberty, just north of Union. He was twenty-six at the time of his arrival, unmarried and had several years in the Army behind him. For the first year in Union, Peter lived in a boarding house run by Ercel and Harry Stewart; the same house where Buddy Savage (Chapter Eight) makes his home today. By the following year, Peter was married, and a year after that he had a family.

For the interview, I sat with Peter in his spacious house, which is well furnished and well kept, at a table next to a large picture window that shares the same view the ancestors have from the cemetery. I could see the casket factory ensconced on the opposite shore of Seven Tree Pond.

"What's it like to come into a town cold turkey to take over a business as the owner's son?" I asked him.

"I didn't let it make a difference. I liked small town living, and I pitched in and said that I was going to make it here." That no-nonsense approach seems to have set the tone for Peter's business career. He looked hard at me, upstraight at the end of the table, well kept.

"I can understand you being busy during the summer, but what did you do during the winter?"

"There were still chores on the land and upkeep. We had warehousing and shipping to do. I don't miss the busy summers. I've been retired from the blueberry business for ten years."

"The business isn't called Monmouth anymore," I said. "Was there a change in ownership?"

He told me that Monmouth was sold to A.L. Stewart in 1965. Then the factory in Portland closed because the State needed the land for the interstate highway. "They decided to sell out rather than relocate," he said. "Then the business was sold again to the Allens in 1983."

"So you worked for three employers. Did that make a difference to you?"

"Not really. The problems were mostly due to the blueberry industry itself."

"Explain that."

"Issues such as the value of the dollar affected our export business. There was competition from the Canadians—and they subsidize their agriculture much more than we do. Then there's problems with out-of-state people moving in and building houses next to the fields, complaining about the use of the herbicides. More and more restrictions make blueberries less of a commodity. There used to be ten blueberry processors in town, now there's only two."

"These are wild blueberries," I said. "Who put them into production originally?" [Blueberries, raspberries and cranberries are the only native fruit in Maine.]

"Up until about fifty years ago, it was mostly Finnish people. They used to have chickens and grow blueberries. But their children didn't stick around because of the lack of jobs. The area wasn't prospering at all."

I remembered an elderly Finnish couple, patients of mine, who retired and sold their large farm under the auspices of a developer. They moved to a small, newer house near the Common. The development group, the members of which tried to keep their identities carefully hidden, split the blueberry land into four-or five-acre parcels and sold it all. Now when you travel up the hill, you see upscale houses planted in the midst of these fields, some of the fields still in production, but most of them not.

"Has any new land been brought into production?"

"No. It's either grown up, or been sold off. The amount of land in production has fallen off, but the tonnage has increased because of newer methods, but we still burn the fields every other year to prune off the old vines and allow the younger ones to bear."

I thought of my own little patch of wild blueberries at the back of our field. I didn't want to use an herbicide, and I decided to use fertilizer. What I got was a patch of thriving weeds with the berries still struggling. It was a moot point, because wild animals ate every one of the berries. I thought the wild turkeys might be at fault. Maine re-introduced the wild turkey to the environment and ever since, herds of the iridescent-feathered birds roam the countryside. I love to see them. I told Peter about the turkeys.

"Turkeys," he scoffed. "A real nuisance. No way to keep them out. They're like seagulls: shovel it in at one end and it comes out the other."

"What happened this year with the low prices?"

"Too much production," he replied.

"Was it difficult to be a manager of a factory and live in the same town where the employees lived?"

"It helped to know the people, and they knew me, but there was a tremendous turnover, since it was seasonal work. We couldn't afford to pay much, and except for a few long-term employees, you didn't know if a worker would be there after lunch or not. It was especially hard in the fall when we picked and processed the squash—seven o'clock in the morning, ice on the floor, cold, wet." He shook his head. "There's not a whole lot of money floating around."

My son raked berries for several years. It's a hard job during the hottest part of the summer, stooping over and scooping up the berries with a short-handled tined shovel device called a rake. The work only lasts a few weeks, but it gives students extra money for school. As of this writing, the going rate to the rakers is ten cents a pound.

"Have you been involved in other types of work in Union?" I asked.

"Driving the school bus. Mostly now, I just fill in. The fire department, of course. When my own kids were small, I saw that there were a lot of kids heading in the wrong direction; so I joined up with the sheriff's department. I stayed with them for twenty-five years."

"Do you have any regrets?"

"I'm happy with this small town living, but I might not have stayed where I am for so many years. It's hard to break loose and change. What I was doing was quite specific and not so transferable elsewhere. And my [two] children live here. They like small towns; their friends are here and both their spouses are from here. It's not a bad area to live in—the schools are good."

"You split with your first wife, and now you're married to Myrna."

"Yes, Myrna used to work for the company. She was in charge of a raking crew."

"You were a very visible member of the community; so was your first wife, Marcia, since she was the town clerk for so many years. People get used to the status quo. Given you worked in town, did you feel many repercussions from the divorce, since this is a small town?"

"If there was any, it wasn't evident to me. People had their opinions, but life went on as usual. Looking back, I could have done more with my kids. I was quite busy most of the time—the summers especially. It's nothing I would recommend to anyone. It's best to spread out work over the whole year."

"It was busy in this house, too. I remember it quite well," I said.

"Believe me, I *know*," replied Peter, quickly. "It cut down on privacy. A bunch of men from New Jersey, drunk, and I wouldn't be able to get supper because they wanted their hunting licenses. But it provided a way of life for my ex-wife, and she didn't have to have a babysitter."

"Sometimes a man is put in the position of having to do what he has to do," I said.

"In my work, there's a right way to do it, and I always tried to do it the right way."

"Does that 'right way' come from philosophy or religion?"

"No. It was *my* way. I watched others and some of them didn't use the best techniques. I had the opportunity to learn a lot, if I kept an open mind."

"Do you think truth is absolute, or is it something that will work itself out over a period of time?"

"The second choice. Truth will work itself out in a lot of ways."

"Is there anything that you feel strongly about, something that really sets you off, in either a good or bad way?"

"I don't feel strongly about anything. I do feel I kept the industry going in the right direction at the time."

"How do you see yourself, as a business man, a farmer or what?"

"As a farmer on our own fields. I had to have the knowledge to do the best practices, which were constantly changing. On the business end, I had to deal with farmers, and if one was losing money, I had to convince him to change practices. I had to get along with them—and some of them were quite rigid."

"There's a considerable amount of responsibility to that job," I said.

"The main pressure was to get all the work done on time. If you made a mistake, that would be *it* for the year—no going back."

"How do you see the future?"

"Agriculture in Maine is becoming more marginalized, and over the next twenty-five years, it's likely to get worse. In Canada, it's the same as here, with small producers and wild blueberries, but I understand that they are clearing 12,000 acres of government land, which they will allow to grow up into berries. That will change things."

"Looks like we will be eating more blueberries," I said, "but not from here."

◆　　　◆　　　◆

About a year after I interviewed Peter, I interviewed Myrna, his wife. I had last seen Myrna when she was with Peter watching the sixth graders play basketball at a local school. Our daughter plays on the same team as Peter's granddaughter. My wife and I were sitting at the top of the bleachers, while Peter and Myrna were several rows below us. My wife leaned over and whispered in my ear, "Hasn't Myrna gained some weight?" I shrugged. I guessed so. I didn't keep tabs.

It turned out that Myrna had gained some weight, because, as we now know, she was pregnant. Peter and Myrna have a daughter, now twelve weeks old, and Myrna has trimmed down considerably. Myrna is rosy and smiling, healthy looking. Peter has a spring to his step, and he looks fifteen years younger.

As I walked into their kitchen I note the baby chair on the table. The house was quiet, but only because the baby was napping. I felt a bit hurried, thinking the baby would waken at any moment, but she didn't.

I started by asking Myrna where she came from originally.

"From Freedom, Montville area," she replied. I left school at fourteen, because I was pregnant with my first child—he's now twenty-six."

"You're a very intelligent lady," I said. "How did you feel, leaving school at that early age?"

"My father was a terrible alcoholic—verbal abuse, mostly—and it was a way out. I didn't care about school. I wanted family life, and I knew that I didn't want my kids to be brought up as I was. Later, I did go back and get my GED."

"Did you get married?"

"Yes, and we had a daughter, now twenty-one. She has cystic fibrosis [CF], and my life was pretty much in a tailspin with her in and out of hospitals and my husband not wanting to help. About that time, I started working for the blueberry company up in Searsmont [north of Union]. Both my ex-husband and I worked there."

"Where is your daughter now?" I asked.

"Living right across the lake. The CF has progressed, but she's getting married in July. Her fiancé is a good guy. She asked Peter to give her away at the wedding." She smiled. [Sadly, since this interview, her daughter has died.]

"Tell me about your working with the blueberry company."

"That started over twenty years ago, and I was doing a variety of things—cutting bushes, burning—and I had a crew. Actually, my husband had the crew and I winnowed [the winnowing machine separates the berries from plant debris]. After the first year, he didn't want to do it; so I took over. I ran a crew of up to 150 people at the Waldo County end of things. Actually, I continued to run the crew until two years ago."

"Why did you stop?"

"The kids today don't have to work anymore. It's sad. It used to be that a good raker could make $125 a day, but now, especially with the younger ones, they have to be paid the minimum wage in case they don't rake up to that amount. Most of the kids aren't used to farm labor, not growing up on a farm. That was the end of an era. Now, nearly all the crews are migrant workers, from Mexico. At the peak of it in the nineties, our crew could out-rake even the professionals [the migrant crews], and we once did half a million pounds in a three-to four-week period. And it was tough, picking up kids in our bus from different small towns. Some of the kids, the parents sent them just so the parents could buy alcohol. To others, it was a way to get out of the house. All different reasons, but always my job to organize."

"When did you meet Peter?"

"I met Peter just before I decided to move down here, because the manager up there died, and we started helping them in Union. I didn't really get to know him Peter until after his marriage died."

"You seem to have a lot in common with Peter," I said.

"We got together probably because I had so little support—especially with my daughter—and he was having his troubles, too. It was a mutual support system."

"What is it like marrying into a town, and marrying a prominent man, with a prominent ex-wife?"

"It's been difficult for a long period. Still some problems left. I didn't feel like I belonged here, and I felt better in a place that was neutral, like at camp. Our camp [near Greenville, Maine] was my salvation. Up there we have a good support group, helpful, non-judgmental—like a second family. As time has gone by here, it's been easier, though."

"What hurt the most?"

"When we would go to a function in town, I felt like the lone rider out. I knew people were talking, and it was uncomfortable. Some people were very supportive, happy for Peter. I think attitudes have changed. At first, I think people thought that I came to get what I could get. And it was the age difference—twenty-nine years—and that was equally hard to accept. But I was not that type of person, and I've never been built like that. I would have left my husband, regardless.

"Now we have the baby, and it wasn't that unexpected. We always knew it was a possibility, but when I reached my fortieth birthday, we figured that I wouldn't have a child. Then two weeks later, I found out I was pregnant. It was a miracle—but nothing figures. How much more evidence do people need?"

"How do you make your decisions in life, the major ones?"

"I look inside myself, and I pray a lot."

"Does that work?"

"Sometimes I need more input from family, friends. Sometimes I get lost—the answers just not being there."

"Yet you seem optimistic," I said.

"Some of that is from having to live for the moment. I learned that having to deal with my daughter's illness, because there were many times when each day could have been her last, knowing only that she will live until her time comes. That all grew me up quickly. I was nineteen when I had her, and I saw that certain things just had to be done. Looking back, I don't even remember being a kid. Peter and our little baby—that's nothing but optimistic."

◆   ◆   ◆

Like many Mainers, Peter is a definite kind of guy. If you ask a question, you will receive an answer, but if you want more elaboration on that answer, you will be given the same answer. I suppose you could call that being down-to-earth, though I am at a loss to find a word in English that properly describes his quality. Myrna rounds things out with her natural openness, probably coming from her difficult life.

Peter's traditional values and his interest in law enforcement reinforce his regard for the "right way." The values of the community matched his values. He denies the effect of the great absolutes of religion, and he appears of a philosophical nature when he says that truth is more relative than absolute. His foundation is the culture of the community. He carried out his life without disruption, even through a high profile divorce in this small community, which only goes to show that his rhythms match the rhythms of the community. He must derive satisfaction from seeing the school bus that he drives sitting in his dooryard.

Since Peter has introduced farming to us, let us next speak with Lee Houghton, who has a dairy farm on the other side of the valley.

14

The Farmer Takes a Wife

Lee Houghton owns a farm on the sharp bend of the North Union Road on Coggin Hill. My wife and I bicycle up that road frequently during warm weather. Two blue silos mark Lee's farm, and the milking house was once an old garage sitting next to my barn. Years ago, I had to move that old garage because I needed to revise my driveway, which was semi-circular and had two entrances at the time. After several collisions involving elderly patients pulling out of my driveway onto the road just below the crest of a hill—none with injuries, thank goodness—I decided to make it a one-entrance drive at the top of the hill. I traded the garage to Lee for a large stack of pine boards cut by Herb Harriman, the subject of a later chapter, and some of these boards are still stored in my barn today.

Lee jacked up the garage by himself, put it on a trailer and pulled it to his property with his tractor, devising a contraption that he attached to the top of the garage deflecting the wires crossing the road. He hauled off the garage, never with the help of anyone.

I interviewed Lee in his old farmhouse kitchen where we sat at the table by the woodstove. From a window, I could look out to his red barn, the field and some cows standing in the mud. Lee is tall, with a well-developed upper body, and though he has a youngish-appearing face, his hair is nearly snow white.

"My wife tells me that you and she raked blueberries together back in grade school." I said.

"Yeah, we did. I remember that." He grinned. "I started raking when I was eight. I don't think they allow that now."

"Did you work in other agricultural ventures while you were young?"

"I fed chickens, helped hay. I had sheep and cattle in high school." Lee looks straight ahead when he answers questions.

"Was it a natural evolution for you to go into agriculture when you went to college?"

"I first went to Unity College [Unity, Maine] in forestry, and I worked for a dairy farmer for room and board. They were the nicest people, so laid back, never got angry. If something would happen to the man, say he got his hat or corncob pipe knocked into the gutter by the swipe of a cow's tail, he would never raise his voice, and he would just pick up his stuff and go back to work. I enjoyed working for them, being there—the whole lifestyle."

"You must have transferred to Orono, because I know you majored in agriculture."

"At Orono I worked at a dairy farm milking cows, and I bagged groceries to get through school," he replied. "During my last summer I went to Massachusetts to try a different line of work, selling encyclopedias. *That's* not a reputable job. You force your way in and do whatever you can to get people to buy the things. Halfway through the first day I knew it wasn't for me. I drove out of Boston and into the country near Concord, and I got a job at Great Brook Farm. There was another fellow working there. I'm still friends with him. He now has his own farm in Vermont."

"What happened after you graduated?"

"Here in Union, I worked at the casket factory."

An old-time Union resident named Pearl Oakes once owned the farm that Lee now owns. I knew about that, especially since the farmhouse that my wife and I bought in the early seventies had been a hangout for Pearl and the previous owner and builder of our house, Frank Lenfest. Frank had died in the late 1930s, and the son of his widow, Henry, had sold us the house a few years after his mother died. Both Frank and Pearl had worked in the barrel stave mill below our house on the St. George River.

"How did you hook up with Pearl Oakes?"

"I met Pearl during my junior year in high school," Lee said. "I bought a side delivery rake off of him. I didn't have enough money at the time, but he let me pay for it a little at a time. His farm was getting pretty run down, and he used to say that it could be a show place if the right person had it, but he would always say that the farm was 'not for sale.' All along, though, he was always encouraging me to farm.

"When I was in college Pearl was living with a family in Thomaston that was helping to take care of him. During my junior year, he got sick and he was afraid he was going to die. Unknown to me, he deeded the farm over to me. The family he was living with got wind of it and they began to put pressure on him to change his decision."

"What happened then?"

"He called me at the university and explained what he had done. By then he wasn't so sick. He wanted me to deed it back over to him to show these people that it was all a lie that I was taking advantage of him. So I did it.

"Pearl knew that after he died, his relatives and friends would not be happy if he just deeded the farm over to me. So he deeded it to Charlena Hall, his niece and friend, and he made a verbal agreement with her that it would go to me if I stayed on the farm for fifteen years. If I left the farm before that, I would get one-fifteenth of the farm for every year that I stayed, and I had to pay the inheritance taxes. Charlena lived here, and I took care of her for three years. Toward the end of it, she needed a lot of care, and I paid a neighbor to come in and help. But she was about to lose her leg, and I had to place her in the nursing home. Shortly after that, she died."

I remember Charlena quite well, because I made house calls on her when she was on the farm. I took care of her until she died. I told Lee that she was a very nice lady.

"I never heard her ever speak ill of anybody," he said.

"How long have you had control of the operation of the farm?"

"Since 1972."

"As a farmer, how do you see your place in the community? Do you feel attacked by people who do not want to live near farming industry, or supported?"

"Both. But the economic aspects overshadow all of that. We are fighting for *survival.*"

"It's that bad?"

"Yes, it's bad. I've been doing this for thirty years. We would get one to two good years, then a half a dozen terrible years. This year was the worst since '77, price-wise." ["Dairy prices have dropped from a high of $19 per one hundred pounds in mid-2001 to an average price of $12.75 in 2002 for the same amount." (*Maine Sunday Telegram*, 12-22-02)]

"Does having these economic difficulties take away from the pleasure in your work?"

"I put it out of my mind. If I'm mowing or planting, I enjoy it, and I can forget about all the problems. My ex-wife said that all I do is work, but I told her that I do other things, for instance, that particular day I was going out to watch my corn grow."

"Does your greatest satisfaction come when the milk truck pulls out of your dooryard full of milk?"

"No, it's the whole thing. I get satisfaction from plowing, the sun, when the corn comes up—trying to get it to come up even, despite the fact that we're using old patched together equipment. I get satisfaction from a barn full of hay, a silo full of corn, and a cellar full of wood. I hope that the place looks a little better every year."

"You use other people's land, do you not?"

"My first few years of farming I used land from eighteen different landowners. Now I farm only my land. It used to be that a farmer could use somebody's land, and the people were glad to have the land kept up, and they didn't put on a lot of restrictions. Now they want half the hay or they don't like to have the fields spread. People forget what farming entails. I got tired of trying to educate the landowners. I might have spent three weeks picking up rocks to have the owner change his mind about the whole thing." [We have a field behind our house from which we allow Bob Whittier, another local farmer, to take the hay. In turn, he keeps up the field nicely. It's a good relationship.]

"You set out to attain a lifestyle. Have you achieved that?"

"Yes."

"Is it lacking anything?"

"Money."

"Anything other than that?"

"No."

"It's odd," I said, "each of the men that I've interviewed who both live and work in town say that earning enough money is hard."

"I could work at MBNA, but I can't see having a person looking over my shoulder. It's bad enough to have the milk inspector every six months. Just all the driving to and from work—that would be stressful. My wife's daughter asked me once how I could stand working alone all the time. I told her if I needed company, I'd go see Leslie Luce [a farmer in North Union]. He has the same problems I have. We can talk."

"So you have some sort of peer group here in town?"

"Yes. For thirty years—and through several wives—I had to fight the conception that I'm not a financial success, but I've nearly accomplished what I set out to do. That's valuable to me, at least."

"What was it you set out to do?"

"Build a viable farm, have all my own land, have my own lifestyle as a farmer—something I could build on year after year and see results from it."

"Sounds like a marriage," I said.

"It is."

"I can see why it would be difficult," I said.

"Yes," he replied, rather glumly. "My first wife said that I was married to the farm; that 99 percent of my energy *went* into the farm." He paused. "One thing about farming, you tend to deal with people that have a different moral sense. I've met a lot of nice people in the line of work I'm in. For instance, I used to buy grain from Erma and Merle Overlock. I dealt with them for forty years, up until they died. I wouldn't deal with anyone else. They were like family. They even backed me financially at one time, and they never asked for the money back, even though I did pay them back."

"Can you characterize the quality you prize in these farming people?"

"Independence," he replied. "They're free thinkers, and they don't go along like a herd of sheep—along with the majority. That gets us in trouble sometimes."

"So many of the men I've interviewed are doing their own things, in a peer group of one, and you are doing that, too; but you have people to relate to."

"I've always said that there's no one right way to farm. One way might be best for one person, but not for the rest. Bob Whittier farms completely different from me, but that may be the only way for him."

"I see a considerable element of creativity in your job."

Lee nods. "It's never boring."

"How many hours a day do you work?"

"Twelve to fifteen."

"Let's say that you have a really good day, and you do things that turn out just right. There's no one to see what you did."

"You have to satisfy yourself. You can't look to others for that satisfaction."

"Isn't it lonely?"

"It can be."

"Yet that dairy farmer you worked for in Unity, where you became enamored with the lifestyle, he had a wife, and they worked together."

"One of the reasons he wanted me to work there was to give his wife a break. The funny thing was—she couldn't stand being left out—she wanted to be out in the barn with him. He thought the world of his wife. They're dead now."

"Does a farm wife need to have grown up on a farm?"

"Anyone who hasn't grown up on a farm will have an unrealistic view of farm life."

"There's so few farmers around here now that it must be difficult to find women who have grown up on a farm."

"Around *here* it's hard," he replied. "Lincoln's [Hawes] wife and Bob Whittier's wife were raised on farms [Gail Whittier is sister to Richard Kirkpatrick from Chapter 7].

"It must be difficult to run a farm all by yourself."

"Almost impossible."

"A catch-22," I said.

"Oh yeah. It takes a special kind of woman to stand me."

"This whole thing is a very unique situation," I said.

"I've always known that—since my first divorce. We never fought, for seven years. Then one day, she went out of state to visit some relatives, and she never came back. I didn't have a *clue*, and I was pretty messed up over it. She said that I was living my dream, not hers."

"How about that friend of yours that worked with you in Mass. and who now has a farm in Vermont, is he married?"

"His marriage has lasted, barely, and somehow they came to an understanding. For a while, she liked it, then she hated it, then she got a job. Last summer she came back to part-time work on the farm, and she continues to work on her own—that seems to satisfy her needs."

I had not yet met Lee's new wife, and I asked, "You just got married. Does your wife have any farm experience?"

"She grew up on a chicken farm in southern Maine."

"That's a beginning," I said. "How did you meet?"

"At the dance—Crystal Falls."

"At the dance" brought up a flash of memories for me. Maine has country and western dances, and they really are fun, if you like that sort of thing and, in the not too distance past if you didn't mind the cigarette smoke. Smoking has since been banned at all public indoor gatherings in Maine. Many romances, licit and illicit, have begun at the dances. In attendance are dudes in cowboy outfits, older couples dancing cheek to cheek, farmers just out from milking, hired men off the farm spending all their money or giving it away, younger couples showing off, drunks insulting everyone. Always BYOB (Bring Your Own Beverage). It's quite the experience just to sit back and watch, but more fun to get into the fray and dance.

"Does your wife work?"

"At MBNA. She says I could get a job there, too."

I laughed. "I can just see you sitting in front of a computer, wearing a tie."

"Somehow, I'm going to weather it. The way I look at it, what choice do I have? I don't want to work for someone. I tried that."

"When was that?"

"You remember when I sold my cows? I quit the farm for six months. First, I went to work at Statler Tissue in Augusta. There, nobody would do more than they absolutely had to. It was unionized, you know, until it went *broke*. I remember one time a machine stopped working, and everyone just stood around doing nothing. I and this other fellow figured we could fix the machine; so we started working on it. Well, we got talked to about *that*—we were supposed to just stand around. That's why they went bankrupt; nobody was willing to work.

"Then I went to work at L.L. Bean for a few months. I saw the difference between a place that was unionized and one that wasn't, but it was still forty hours of boredom, no goals, no satisfaction—other than the paycheck. Most people didn't care about their work."

The phone rang, and Lee talked to someone about heifers for about five minutes. When he returned, I asked him if he had anything else he wanted to say.

"I guess I'm not perfect. I haven't done everything just right, especially my marriages, but a person never gets anywhere if he gives in to setbacks. I have to try again and again. I'm pretty outspoken, and I say things that other people don't want to hear. They get upset. That's the reason I withdrew from the town meetings. Even if I have a good idea, nobody will listen if they don't like where it's coming from. I don't have the ability of a politician."

"Why do you think you are doing what you are doing?"

"Pearl had hopes of what I could do here. Charlena wanted me to succeed, and the Overlocks helped me in all sorts of ways. When I asked the Overlocks about the money I owed them, they said that they considered it an investment in me." He choked up with that last word.

"Explain that a bit more?" I asked.

"I suppose they wanted me to help finish what they got started, maybe part of their going on after they died—their investment in me."

"Did that give you a sense of mission?"

"Yeah." He thought for a moment. "I still look back at their pictures. I cared a lot for those people. I would hate to disappoint them. Sounds stupid, since they're all dead."

"There's a lot tied up in this," I said. "There's the personal connection—much like family, there's the lifestyle that you want to maintain, there's an element of mission. Is there something more here, something transcendent?"

"All these people have died, and I'm the product of their hopes."

"Their ideals?"

"Yes. But more than that. It's the love they had for me. It's a manifestation of the enduring quality of love."

I had to end with that.

◆   ◆   ◆

Most of us lead lives more or less balanced with work, family and other interests. Lee's entire life heavily tilts toward his work. That is a personal preference, and he has paid the price in divorces and the consequent upheavals.

Someone like Lee makes me walk away from the interview shaking my head. His life consists of work and the land, primarily. If he were to stop working, as Pearl had to do because of his age, then everything comes apart, and within a few years, the land would grow up with alders, with the farm falling in. A post and beam barn begins to sag at the ridgepole, and then in a few years, the roof collapses in the middle. The walls remain upright, but over the years they, too, begin to tumble in toward the middle. It's a pile of rotting lumber heaped into a cellar with a stone foundation. Easier to burn it rather than haul the mess away. The local volunteer fire department will monitor the fire using it for training.

After the families fight about who is going to do what about the land, the land will be sold at a good price and all the family members divvy up the proceeds. Soon enough we see a new house, constructed in the New England fashion and positioned in the place of the best view, whereas the farm before had been built conveniently close to the road. We turn around twice and that house is for sale. The new people decided they really didn't want to live in Maine. It's so far from family, and how can anybody stand those blackflies and mosquitoes during the spring, and what about those long winters, the dull, gray autumn and that dratted mud season in March? March mudness. The best of it, as Lee says, is to go into the field and watch the corn grow.

The farmer is a light person. The most important aspect in his life is the sun. The sun gives life and energy to all of us, and we can nod our heads with that fact. Of all of us, though, the farmer most directly depends on the sun. He thinks about it every day. What does that do to a person?

I wanted to ask Lee that question—about light. I drove to his house on a late Sunday morning when the milking was done. We again sat in the kitchen, but this time, I asked his wife, Linda, to be present. Lee and Linda married two years ago. She's a thoughtful woman, contemporary to Lee, with abundant grayish curly hair and a kind face. Dressed in a checkered shirt and work pants, she sat quietly at the table as I first talked with Lee.

"You are totally dependent upon the weather in your life, dependent basically on the sun. How does that affect you as a person?" I asked.

"Simply, I have to do the best I can with what's dealt me," Lee replied. "I might have a great crop, and in two nights army worms could clean out a whole field. I have to look to the future. There's never enough feed on hand. Merle taught me that. If he had an excess of feed, he wouldn't sell it that year, because the next year might be a bad one."

"But how does that change or mold you as a person? Does having to plan ahead and deal with the vagaries of nature reflect in your personal life?"

"It doesn't make any difference. The people like the Overlocks and Charlena, the love that they had for me, *that* carried me through, and I'd be a different person had I not met them. Maybe my first two wives would have benefited had I changed before that."

"Still, I don't understand what it feels like to have to mold one's behavior to the weather." I said.

"You learn to deal with it. When I was younger, I used to get angry when the hay got rained on. But there's nothing I can do about it. In *your* life," and he looked at me, "you have to deal with difficult people—people out of your control—and it might make you angry. It's the *same* thing."

"You change what you can change and accept what you can't," interjected Linda. Lee nodded.

"Then having to deal with the weather, as an aspect of your life, is part of the professionalism of being a farmer," I said. They both nodded firm agreement. "Lee, how about the political aspects in your life—having to deal with *people?*"

"I'm still working on that," he replied with a grim smile.

"Linda, how does it affect your life that you are so dependent on the weather?" I asked.

"You have to be one with the weather. By farming, you are closer to nature, but I grew up on a farm, and that feeling has always been with me. I'm generally pretty accepting, especially about people's differences."

"She balances me in that regard," Lee added.

"Linda, you were born on a farm?"

"My father, when he was in the Navy, bought a farm in Windham [Maine] from an ad in the paper without even seeing it. So my mother and the rest of the family moved to the farm—while he was still on a ship somewhere—and she learned to milk the cows, dress the chickens. Eventually my father retired from the Navy, and he became a full-time farmer, and turned it into a commercial poultry business."

"Tell me about your mother and what it was like to move to a farm cold tur-key, so to speak?"

"It was an adjustment. You see, my mother grew up in Portland, and she was elegant, gorgeous. She and my two sisters and my brother—I wasn't yet born—moved to the farm in Windham and found all the pipes frozen. It was so cold and dark, and they were scared. They all spent the first night in the same bed upstairs. But with the neighbors' help, she learned to run the farm."

"Sounds like *The Egg and I*," I said.

Linda smiled. "She relates to that."

"What happened when the poultry business crashed?"

"Then he sold it and worked for an oil company."

"Did you go to school after high school?"

"I went one year at the Portland School of Art, and after that year, I thought that I could do art on my own. Pretty soon I was doing less and less art."

"What did you end up doing?"

"For the most of my employment, I was an insurance agent. When I got mar-ried, I stayed home to take care of the kids. I worked part-time in a library."

"Where do you work outside the farm now?"

"MBNA in Rockland."

"Is that a 'have to' job?"

"If I could add as much working here on the farm, then I would farm full-time. I can contribute more by working outside. My employment benefits pro-vide health insurance and even a scholarship for Lee's daughter."

"It seems that people who own farms around here have few choices," I said. "They can be poor, or they can try to expand to take advantage of larger scale—with all the problems that such a move entails; or, as in your case, some-one has to work outside the farm to keep it all going."

Her smile turned crooked. "I know. My daughter is trying to farm—raising vegetables. She's down on the Skidmore Road on one of Lee's other properties. She's researched it and has an idea of how large a business she would need to suc-ceed. At this point, she needs a second job as well."

"So how are things working out with you two and the farm, especially with all the problems related to dairy farming now days?"

"I like Union and the farm," she replied, "and I know that Lee will manage. He has the tenacity to deal with whatever comes his way. Receiving a fair price for milk would help."

"What do you think, Lee?"

He thought for a moment. "I think that the farm will grow to the extent that we as a couple grow. Either you grow, or you grow apart. I know that when I start in a direction I shouldn't be going in, then I listen to her, because she usually doesn't say much, but when she does, I listen—especially if it's something people-related. Then I listen."

15

Idyllic Life

If we walk down the hill from Peter Soule's house to another bridge over the St. George River, we come to Ayer Park, a picnic and swimming area with a boat ramp. The Union mini-triathlon was once held in this area each summer; the proceeds of which went to the Union Elementary School and its international program, each class focusing on a different country. Though the event always had plenty of entrants, interest waned, especially with the divorces of two of the couples from the group of five couples that put it together.

The running part of the event went farther down the road beginning at the bridge, turning onto Come Spring Lane, a dirt road to the right. A short distance down Come Spring Lane, we traverse the dooryard of Herb Harriman's farm. To the left is his sawmill with neatly stacked pine lumber, and to the right, his old farmhouse overlooking a field with Round Pond in the distance. Two large friendly dogs make it appear that they are guarding the place. Sturdy fences, built for the love of horses, come nearly to the house.

The connection to Herb comes from my own barn. You might recall that I traded a small building to Lee for lumber. Herb cut the lumber for Lee with his portable mill. Today was a cold, snowy day, and Herb and I sat in their comfortably decorated living room toasted warm by a woodstove. Two large pillows for the dogs sprawled empty in front of the television set.

I knew that Herb was originally from Union, because I had taken care of both his parents, now gone. The family had lived in Massachusetts while his father taught English, but they spent the summers in Union. His mother had helped set up the town library, and his grandfather owned the gas station, when it *was* a station, where Ken Rogers now has his auto trim shop. Herb's great-grandfather was the station master at the train depot in Union, now the blueberry factory. Herb felt misplaced during the years they lived in Massachusetts.

In his late sixties, Herb appears younger, moves around well, but it's his open and earnest demeanor that lends an appearance of youth, though he does have a dark gray beard. He speaks with impeccable grammar. I asked him how he saw life when he was in high school in Massachusetts.

"I wanted to be a dairy farmer. At the time, I thought it was realistic."

"How did you become interested in that?"

"We lived in a semi-rural area, and I worked on a dairy farm as a kid. I never cared about city or suburban life. Besides, I preferred working on a farm, with the cows. I liked people—but only in small doses."

"What did you do after high school?"

"I went to the University of Massachusetts for one year in animal husbandry. But my plans for being a dairy farmer went out the window. After that, I didn't give a damn, and I was disgusted with the whole area; so I took off, mostly on a motorcycle to see the country—that was 1954."

"Sounds like a turning point in your life," I said.

"I guess I was always one that if I had a plan, and the plan went awry, then I would get bent, because I don't like being disappointed. Now, my wife does the planning. If I do make a plan, then I always have an alternative, something to fall back on."

"So you took off on your bike. I know you're still interested in them. How did that interest begin?" [Herb on his Harley is a common sight during summer.]

"My father liked motorcycles. I can remember when I was very young. If I didn't want to go to bed, he would sit me in his hands in front of him, as if I were sitting in the seat of a motorcycle, and he would make a noise like an engine and run up the stairs to my bed. That thrilled me. I can remember always running to the window if I heard a bike outside."

"What happened when you returned from your travels?"

"I had the draft breathing down my neck. If had gone back to school I could have avoided the draft. More on an impulse than anything, I joined the Army—three years, mostly in Germany. When I returned, I got married."

"Married? Was it with someone you had known all along?"

"No, I had met her through some friends in New Hampshire."

"So you had to settle down."

"I thought that was what I was supposed to do."

"You must have had to go to work," I said.

"I worked as a truck driver for a few years, and then in 1962 I bought this place and we moved here and started a chicken farm."

"There was a big push for chickens back then," I said.

"Yeah, if I had done what everyone else was doing, I'd still be in the hole today. It was the oil crunch that put it out. With chickens up here, everything had to go with oil."

Herb was speaking of the government's efforts to encourage Mainers to dive into the chicken business. Back then, it was considered the economic savior for Maine workers out of work from dying mills. The chicken barns sprung up quickly with government supported loans, and soon, the market was glutted with chickens, and the price collapsed, just as overhead costs escalated because of the rising price of oil. Out went the chicken industry, leaving barns full of chicken manure—and no chickens—scattered about the state. Those barns not torn down are barely standing today.

"What happened to your barn?" I asked.

"I kind of kick myself for tearing it down. I had it built; I guess I should have kept it, despite the extra taxes."

"So you lost your primary source of income, and you must have had your three kids by then?" He nodded. "Then what did you do?"

"I went back to what I knew best—driving truck—a tractor trailer for Crowe Rope. I also worked on the town road crew, though I didn't like the job, but I liked the town road commissioner, Gid Winchenbach. It was my way of treading water until I figured out what to do."

"How did you get into the sawmill business?"

"I was always fascinated with sawmills, and I thought a fellow could make it in this area with a portable mill—go right to the customer's property, and do a good job of it. I did that for a year, but I came to the conclusion that I was better off to set up here and have logs brought to my place. Being portable had its problems—especially if I forgot something—but more than that, I was on *their* turf, and I had to do what *they* wanted, even though sometimes it wasn't the best thing to do in my judgment. Now with my own place, sometimes there's plenty of work; other times, I really have to scratch."

"You seem to like working on your own."

"I liked tractor-trailer driving, too. Once I left town, driving a rig, I felt as if I were on my own. That's different than doing delivery work, where you are always under someone's thumb. I always wanted to be on my own—maybe having to live with my father had something to do with that. He was an authoritarian and a disciplinarian."

"Did you find yourself using the same methods that your father used when you had your own children?"

"One day I said to myself, You didn't like it when you were a kid, so lay off."

"Did you?"

"I did," he replied sadly, "but it may have been a bit late with my son, the oldest. The kids still live in the area though, and my son, up until recently, helped me in the mill, but not now, because there isn't enough work. All in all, it took me a long time to grow up."

"You divorced," I said.

"Some people can get married early and do okay, but I don't think I was mature enough. The girls stayed with their mother and Paul with me."

"How did you learn about running and building a sawmill?"

"I read. And I'm not afraid to ask questions—I learned that from my father. In fact, I learned *a lot* of things from him. Things keep cropping up, and I ask myself, Where did that come from? He was my continuing education, I guess. Anyway, I started off with a little building, then added a larger one, then I bought a larger saw, a planer, an edger, trailers."

"How long have you and Vicki been married?"

"Twenty-eight years. She's taught nursing most of that time." [No children in their marriage.]

"Do you have a goal in life?"

"Stay breathing, keep my head above water, enjoy myself. Enjoying myself isn't quite the same as when I was *younger*."

"Does fear play any part in your life?"

"Things are a whole lot different now—geared up to a fast pace, which I don't think is healthy—physically or economically. I just can't see getting all keyed up just so the guys at the top don't have to take a cut in salary. They walk on the tops of the others, just to get what they want."

"It sounds like fairness is important to you."

"Yes. That developed as I got older. I would rather have a good reputation in being honest and fair, rather than otherwise. Kids have a problem today with finding people to look up to. The leaders, the clergy, teachers, the cops—the kids know that so much of what they say is hypocritical bullshit."

"What kind of a foundation is important?" I asked.

"A good human example," he replied.

"Something beyond humans?"

"No. Then the world fights over who's the *best* example."

"Parents?"

"Start with that, but that's hypocrisy on my part. I'm not the best example. I really didn't mature until I turned fifty. I know that kids should have responsibilities, more than just computers, homework and sports."

We sat quietly for a few moments. "When I look at your life," I said, "I see lots of neat things—not only this beautiful place, but also that you are doing what you want, and in the way that you want to do it. Yet I also detect uneasiness, as if you are right on the edge, and things can go all to hell very quickly. Is that how it is? Maybe it's something inherent in this type of lifestyle?"

"I have friends who have worked for big corporations all their lives, and now they're well retired, where I'm not."

"Does that bother you?"

"I learned a long time ago never to envy anyone. I had a friend growing up, and he had everything. Then he died—young. Better off being myself."

"Then where does this uneasiness come from?"

"It's recent, because more people are moving in, taxes going up. Something's *wrong* with the picture. It seems a shame that people can't live in their homes without having to worry about keeping them."

"For me to look at this place, and what you do, it all seems so peaceful," I said.

He shook his head. "With the temperature as low as it is, my work comes to a standstill."

"So you are under the gun a bit."

"I've got to keep my eye open, and I have to wonder about what to do next if things fail. Age is a factor, too. I'm not taking the chances I might have in my forties or fifties."

"Would you say you have to be creative? Maybe that isn't the right word."

"I have to be a jack-of-all-trades. In my business, and especially when I had the chicken business, I couldn't keep calling somebody. And I don't like to do things half-baked. They've taken a lot of things away from us."

"What do you mean? Can you give me an example?"

"I always had respect for shade tree mechanics. With cars as they are, now you can't do that sort of stuff. I miss it."

"So it's not as if you live in your own world, isolated. World events do make their effect here."

"Maybe I should turn off the TV and stop getting the *Bangor Daily News*," he said, and grinned. "It's the trickle-down effect, as with that paper mill closing in Millinocket. It's not just the workers; it's the stores, the property values, the railroad." [From the *Maine Sunday Telegram* the day before this interview, Jan. 19, 2003: "Every paper mill job lost leads to the loss of another 3.4 related jobs."

"Rather than a trickle-down effect," I said, "it sounds more like a gush. The paper today said that the mill closing would result in the loss of more than 3,000 jobs."

"That's why I was always skeptical of MBNA," he continued. "A lot of that happened pretty quickly, and if they pulled up stakes, where would that put us? I'm not a moralist, but their money is made on people's ill judgment."

"How you carry out your business is important to you," I said. "But I think that necessarily puts you on the knife's edge. It really depends on how a person defines success. As with many of the other interviewees, it's difficult to define success when the financial aspect is so deflated around here. Most people think that just because a person makes a lot of money that he or she is successful."

"My father always used to say that there were other types of greatness," Herb said, sadly.

◆   ◆   ◆

Vicki, Herb's wife, was born on a farm in Alna, Maine, when farmers brought the hay loose into the barn. Nowadays, farmers have machines that twirl the equivalent of nine bales of hay into large rolls and cover it with tight, white plastic. The kids call these huge rolls marshmallows. Vicki's family later moved to a farm in Rockville, near Rockland, where her mother, in her eighties, still lives.

Now fifty-six years old, Vicki finds herself working nearly full-time as a pediatric nurse at the hospital in Augusta. I asked her if that was what she wanted to do.

"I would rather be a full-time farmer," she replied firmly.

Vicki has the rosy cheeks of one not afraid to work outside in harsh weather, clear eyes and hair returning nicely after her chemotherapy. It was summer, and we were sitting outside at a picnic table with a view of Round Pond across their cleanly shorn hayfield.

"What were you like in high school?" I asked.

She glanced at the sky, then at me, wanting to be exact. "I was studious, quiet—a beanstalk. It took me two years to get on the field hockey team because I was too thin. I was pretty serious. Even growing up, I didn't have many girl toys. I didn't complain, though. Boys were my playmates. I didn't do any dating until my senior year. My parents brought me up to take responsibility seriously early on and to do a good job."

"How is a person brought up to be like that?"

"I was the oldest daughter. I was given responsibility: babysitting, cooking, changing diapers. My mother passed those responsibilities on to me."

"What about the others in the family?"

"They mostly backed off and let me do it. It was quite an experience."

"And after high school?"

"I did a three-year program in nursing in Salem, Mass. My parents didn't have much money, what with eight kids. After that, my boyfriend and I took off to California—that was in the late sixties. He worked in a silver mine, and we lived in a camper. We were married out there. My parents insisted on that. We came back to the East Coast to buy a dilapidated 300-acre farm in Nova Scotia. I worked on the farm and as a nurse, and he had a job as third mate on the Prince of Fundy [the car ferry that connects southern Nova Scotia to Portland, Maine]."

She sighed. "He found a girlfriend and split. I came back to Maine and had a place in Lincolnville with three horses. I met Herb through the horse club at the Union Fair. We married the next year…. We had the same interests and a love for the land, and he was pretty persistent. That was thirty years ago." She shook her head and smiled faintly at how long ago that was.

"Has it been a hard life?"

"It's not been easy. When he was trucking, I was teaching full-time, but I was able to do the chores. Financially, we needed to do it—*had* to do it. We thought the sawmill through, and we did it. At least we've been able to stay above water and keep the place. I started back to school while he was setting up the sawmill, and I was still working full-time. That was tough, but I'm glad I did it. It was hard caring for his mother, too. [She died five years ago.]

"Then four years ago I was diagnosed to have bipolar disorder. Herb was a good caregiver, and I was put on some meds. Things evened out. Then last year I was diagnosed with lymphoma. Herb became the caregiver again. But now, life's going along pretty well."

"Did you think you were going to die with this last illness?"

She nodded. "I decided to cut back, get rid of stress. It was one of those assessments: Do we sell the farm to make life easier? We both figured that what we do is what we love. So we stayed here. Before we do anything major, we talk it out. I respect his advice—he's that much older than I."

Sitting at their picnic table and taking in the expanse of beauty, which is their farm, the rail fences, the view, the animals, I had to remark that the whole setup looks idyllic.

She shook her head. "I don't sit down and say I'm going to do nothing. Whatever direction I look, there's something to do. We don't take a day off."

"Don't you even go to the Union Fair?" I asked.

"We'll take six hours and go to the Fair this year with our one and only grandson, Josh. Sure, life here is idyllic—through hard *work*, struggling. Added to that, our valuation doubled with the shore frontage and all. Like we're being punished for living here. Fortunately, we've saved some money. We're okay."

"So the whole fantasy of living off the land is just that, a fantasy," I said. "You've had to continue working to supply a steady income."

"It's definitely the way it's become. You can't do it unless you've won the Megabucks." [Vicki's reference is to the owners of the neighboring farm, who, in reality, did win the Megabucks—$6 million. The only difference between before and after the winnings is the make and year of the car parked in the dooryard.]

She paused in thought, and then smiled. "That's not to say we haven't had great times here, too. This place has allowed me to live out my passion: raising and training Morgan horses. We name them after characters in *Come Spring*—Ben Ames Williams's novel. We've traveled…" She nodded her head in thought. "Yeah, we've had some great times."

"Did you consider having a family?"

"Herb had his three children from before. We tried. Nothing happened. I had a workup in Mass. It sort of dropped out of the picture. I felt we would make the best of what we've got. I always had a love for children, and we do a lot around here with kids and the farm, the nieces and nephews. Herb didn't want to adopt."

"How do you look to the future?"

"I'm always one to plan ahead. We're both getting older. Herb says that he wants to die here. I see our life as becoming more peaceful. But the world is in conflict. How much do we want to bring that in? We have a nephew that just returned from Iraq. We all went to meet him at the Jetport. I realized that I hadn't been to Portland for *two* years."

"So you have to insulate yourselves?" I asked.

"The outside interferes with balance—a very fine balance—mentally and physically. I have to keep that in mind."

◆   ◆   ◆

Many people who consider moving to the country think that they would have to make too many compromises. Herb does not compromise in his work, but he does not have the goal to make lots of money—he wants to "get by." Such a goal sets him apart from some of his out-of-state friends who have already retired following thirty years of dedicating their vigor to Lockheed or somesuch, suppressing their own dreams, if they had any, even though those dreams might have led to failure. Now we see Herb and Vicki with water just below their chins. When they're on the edge, can they feel successful? The concept of success really does not apply here.

Living on the edge is not so comfortable, but without it, I know that I feel a lack of something happening. Fat and happy or lean and hungry—it's not an either/or proposition, but more in the tone of moderation. Still, that bit of uneasiness remains. Gotta live with it, can't live without it. Creativity has a lot to do with it.

The weather rules. Lee, the farmer, would agree with that. The weather keeps us on edge all the time, always changing, from hour to hour. We can't plan, or if we do, we must face disappointment. Herb Harriman knows about planning. People may move here for what they think is the easy life, but they don't remain here for that. Relaxing in the yard will likely result in multiple bites, but there are moments of greatness, as Vicki attests. Periods of melancholy may follow periods of happiness, but moments of greatness have no following. And yes, the weather has a lot to do with the edge, that uneasiness. It's part of it, an essential part, but without it, by some mysterious process we find that we are losing control, losing the control to create our lives.

16

The Doctor Is In

For the last interview, we return to the Common and enter Oakside Video to talk with Carol Scott. Carol moved to Union with her family when she was nine years old. She attended local schools and was in the second graduating class in the new high school—now the *old* high school, at least according to my kids. She was a cheerleader in junior high and a basketball player in high school, but according to Carol, she preferred to stay in the background.

Carol is now in her fifties with a young attitude, perhaps because she has raised four children and also because kids are always stopping to talk with her at the video store on the Common where she works. The store isn't overly busy, but it's the only one in town, and if you drive by at night, you can see Carol behind the counter leaning forward in close conversation with a lingering client, young or old. The Common is dark at night, and the light coming from the front windows of the video store welcomes like a solitary beacon. Always someone there to listen.

I asked Carol what her plans were back in high school.

"I always wanted to be an English teacher," she replied.

"What happened?"

"I got married in high school in my senior year." Carol's matter of fact way of talking about herself lends an air of safety. The setting was incongruent: the poor fluorescent lighting, the old wooden flooring, the ancient high ceilings and a wall of black plastic video containers looming behind Carol and rows of colorful video jackets displayed behind me. I was sitting on a stool on the customer side of the counter next to a bowl of candy for sale, while she stood—unwilling to sit—doing a few odd jobs while she talked, but stopping often to look me in the eye and answer a question. She has a broad body and face, and a wide but thin knowing smile, as though she understands maybe more than we think.

"So you started a family early. What happened after high school?"

"I had been working since I was fourteen as a dishwasher at Elmer's. I ended up cooking there. I worked there twenty-five years, and during that time I had my four children."

"Was there any retirement program or anything?"

"No. Nothing. Not even a gold watch."

"What does Randy [her husband] do for work?"

"He used to work at Barker's Garage, but now at BIW [Bath Iron Works, the shipbuilding business in Bath and Maine's largest employer]."

"I remember you got done at Elmer's when it changed owners, but what did you do then?"

"Since we live across the road from the school, for several years, I babysat for some of the teachers. After that, I started work here."

"What's it like working here?"

"Like being a bartender."

"What do you mean?"

"For instance, yesterday, I was opening up, had the door open and just taking my coat off, and this lady comes in and says that she's never been here before. I asked her if she lived here, and she said not by choice, and then she proceeds to tell me her life story. Her husband was abusive. She said she needed someone to talk to. After quite a while talking, she saw a customer coming in, and she left…. I even have a ninety-two year old man who comes in for porn—and he still drives."

"How about kids, do they want to talk?"

"I get a lot of high school students. Three of them come in every Saturday night. One's from a broken home and one complains that her mother is horrible, but mostly they just shoot the breeze. One boy comes in nearly every day and talks about the girl sitting behind him, that he wants to take her out. Then I point out to him that his fly's undone. He turns red and says, 'Oh, my God, do you think she saw it?' I know his father, too, and I can say the apple doesn't fall very far from the tree."

"What do you think of living and working in town?"

"The pay's crap. But it's convenient, and I'm available to help with the grand-kids."

"That seems the way with all the people I've interviewed," I said.

She exhaled. "I went to school with the owner. I was in Florida vacationing, and I got a call that she wanted me, in particular, to work here right *then*, because she wanted someone that she could trust." [Since this writing, Gary Sukeforth, the owner of the grocery store, has bought the business.]

"Do you think the people that live and work in town are a different breed? Are you different in some way?"

"You still have to do a good day's work. I'm not materialistic. I'm happy with my life. I can pay my bills. Look at Will [our youngest son]—he has a sense of happiness." I remembered that Will asked me to say hello to Carol when he learned that I was going to interview her this evening.

"You say you are not materialistic. How do you think that came about?"

"My grandmother raised me. My mother was a party animal. My grandmother didn't have much and didn't want much, just the basics."

"Does that fit in with any philosophic or religious framework with you?"

"I'm just cheap. My happiest moment is going to the grocery store with all my coupons and not having to pay much money."

"That's being frugal," I said.

"I don't know," she replied. "I'll go all the way into Subway in Rockland with a coupon, because I like the challenge of clipping out the coupon. I suppose I lose that much in gas just to get there. Still, I don't drink and I don't smoke. I guess I've got to do something."

"Would you say you lead a simple life?"

"Boring, maybe."

"Are you bored?"

"I do the same thing every day."

"Are you doing what you want?"

"Yeah. Too much confusion is not good for a person. I do lead a simple life. I stay away from groups. My family gave me a fiftieth surprise birthday party, and I thought I was going to kill 'em."

"Are you happy?"

"On a good day, yeah."

"There's something that I'm not getting at," I said.

"I told you I wouldn't be easy." [Carol told me this when I originally asked her for an interview.]

"You're intelligent," I said.

"Thank you."

"Has anyone ever told you that you were intelligent?"

"No."

"If they did, would you listen to them?"

"Being raised in not the best of situations, you kind of don't believe what people tell you. You build a shell around you."

"Do you still have a shell?"

"Oh, God, *yes*," she exclaimed. "That's why I can be friendly but not that *close* to anyone—no girlfriends. I don't hang out."

"Yet, you're a good listener."

"Yeah. I'm always seeing people that have bigger problems than me."

"Do you find it valuable to hear other people's problems and explore their lives?"

She nodded yes.

"Do you intervene in other people's lives, or just listen?"

"I have to put in my two cents worth—even with my grown kids—I have to do that. For instance, there's this pretty girl from Appleton that comes in, and she has this thing that she won't take her shirt off to have sex with her husband because of the white streaks on her belly after her last kid. Maybe she *has* some scars, but she's pretty, not fat, and I keep telling her that there's not a thing wrong with her. So she's now saying that she'll try, and I told her I would keep at her until she did."

"You remind me of Lucy at her psychiatry booth in Peanuts."

"Yeah," she replied.

"You probably do a lot of good for these people who talk with you."

"I hope I do."

"Is that your role in life, to help?"

"If something goes wrong in the family, they call me. My role in life is to help—listening, giving them a shoulder to cry on."

"How can you have a shell and do that?"

"I'm listening to *their* problems."

"Have you ever told any person *your* problems?"

"Nah. I keep everything inside."

"Does that make you nervous?"

"No. Living with my grandmother, I learned that if I kept quiet, I wouldn't get in trouble. But I have to take time out, to veg out, and not have anything to do with people."

"It sounds to me that you have made the perfect life for yourself."

"Yeah."

"Have you ever thought that?"

"Some days, maybe. I could do better, more money, better cars, but I have a nice home. Yeah. I guess this is the perfect life for me."

"I wonder how many people can say that?"

"Not many. Here in Union, I see people I know. In Rockland, that's a whole new territory, and I'm not so comfortable out of my realm."

"Maybe it's comforting for you to know what's going on in this town, and the more you know about this community and its people, the better, as if it's some sort of mystery that needs to be solved."

"It's comfortable," she replied. "It used to be that everybody talked at the post office. Not so much, now. It's called being 'nosy'."

"This video store has become a sort of community center," I said, "but it seems more than that."

"That lady, yesterday, I told you about, she said that I had such a kind face, and she said she needed to talk with somebody."

"This is like putting a picture together," I said. "You are creating something, and you could not be doing this, whatever it is, in any other way than how you are doing it."

That ended the interview for today, but I told her that I wanted to think about this interview for a few days, and then maybe talk some more.

As I was going out the door, Carol began to question me about what I was doing, and I found myself talking about myself for ten minutes or so. A good interviewer, she is. She would have made a great psychologist, but then again, that's what she's doing now, and she doesn't carry the burden of having to be someone's doctor. I guess you could call it a very useful hobby—learning about people.

I wanted to finish the interview, and I especially wanted to know, since she intervenes with suggestions regarding people's lives, how and from where do these suggestions originate? For instance, psychologists generally deal with problems within a conceptual framework that they believe in. Their interventions mostly stay within the realm of that conceptual framework.

It was 8 p.m. several days later, and the "Closed" sign hung on the door. The red milk crate sat under the old mail slot on the door to catch after hour returns. The setting was the same, and I asked her how she responded to people when they presented their problems. What did she use as a guideline?

"Common sense," she replied without hesitation.

"But doesn't the fact that you respond to these people's problems get you involved with them in some way?"

"No. I can stay outside, not involved, and since I don't like getting that close to people, I can stay *objective*. They know I'm not going to try to run their lives."

"It still seems to me that you would be developing some sort of ongoing relationship."

"Not really. There might be a boyfriend problem one day, and then the next day it would be having trouble with a teacher. I can tell if someone is having a down day, and I'll ask, 'What's the matter?' It's easy to tell when they need to talk, and besides, they don't have to pay me anything."

"Are you creative?"

She thought for a while. "No, not at all."

"You don't think that what you do is creative?"

"If you mean creating an atmosphere where people can spill their guts—if *that's* what you mean—then, yes, probably."

"Are you ambitious?"

"I'm not lazy."

"Are you striving for something?"

"I'm not looking for greener pastures."

"Do you find that people and their problems seem to fall into some kind of general groupings. And you might say to yourself, 'Oh, here it comes again?'"

She turned to me. "Don't you find in your work that each person is interesting, that each person is different?"

"Yeah," I replied. "But we doctors have to put people's quirks and problems into categories, into diagnostic groups, and attach a code to it, or else we don't get paid. That means we have to see people and their problems within the eyes of the very people who design the diagnostic handbook."

Carol shook her head, and tightened her lips.

That ended the interview, but I suddenly saw why Carol liked our teenaged son, Will, so much. She mentioned him at the beginning of the interview and said he had a sense of happiness. Will was born in India, and because of prematurity and malnutrition at birth, as well as two blood-borne infections immediately after he was born, he has learning disabilities. The greatest disability is that he cannot use logic, and some memory problems accompany that. I have learned a great deal from Will because of his lack of ability to use logic. Without logic, a person cannot form a conceptual framework, and that prevents seeing the "big picture." Without a big picture, all information coming in appears as unique information and does not fit into preconceptions.

Will takes people as they are. He does not face each person in his world with a preconceived prejudicial viewpoint. You would never hear Will call someone a name, such as a jerk, because that implies a conceptual framework that the person is a jerk, and the person just confirmed that prejudgment once again. Will does not understand cynicism. He thinks it's cruel and unfair when he hears it, and I think he is correct. So he takes each person as he or she comes at that moment. People enjoy that, and consequently, he is popular at school. In fact, just recently, even though he is in the special education program, he was voted student of the month in his high school.

I have learned from Will to begin to extract myself from diagnostic categories and become less clinical, which is difficult for me—and probably most doctors, because of the way we are trained. Carol spotted that, and as I was about to leave, she asked me why I was so "clinical" all the time. She, in fact, used *that* word. I was flustered by the question.

I gave a rather weak answer, "When I'm doing these interviews, I can't put too much of my emotional self into the interviews, because I am interested in what the interviewee feels in the most true and unbiased way."

"Sure," she replied, "but you're even like that when you come in to get a movie with Will."

What could I say?

The point is that Carol must look at each situation much as Will does in order to do what she does, even though she has no learning disabilities. That's why she and Will have a bond, and she bonds (though she would rather *die* than use that word) with other people in town. I think that Carol is creative in that she fashions a response to each of the people she encounters based on his or her particular individuality. Everyday life is more creative without preconceived conceptional frameworks—prejudices. If she had gone to college, and if it turned out that she went into counseling of some sort, would Carol then have all the preconceived clinical frameworks in dealing with her clients as do nearly all therapists? Who can answer that? One thing is for sure, Carol functions as another of the truth outposts in town, as does the wife of Mike the postmaster, Jennifer; Bonnie, also at the post office; and my own wife, Dianne. Carol is on the Common—and "after hours." Most convenient.

My hunch about Carol, and using her for the last interview, proved correct. She personifies in a nice way those sorts of characteristics that make a person want to live and work in the same town.

17

Conclusions

The people in this book crowd into your head, and simply putting them there can touch off something. For me, I can't call it philosophical, because if I come to some sort of philosophical conclusions, chances are good I have selected whatever I want from the interviews which I would use to bolster my conclusions. Anyone could prove just about anything that way, but such is the method we generally use in our everyday experiences. Do we suppose that the conclusions we draw from our own experiences are the only proper conclusions that can be drawn, and what we saw was all there was for anyone to see? I hope not, even though I still believe these people have something important to tell us within the realm of philosophy.

You have read about a multitude of values from different people, and on the surface, it seems that the only thing they have in common is that they have chosen to both work and live in one town, Union. Yet, there remains a process working beneath. I can't exactly call it an equation, but there remains a process, and the values placed in this process are the values of these people.

As people would say, this is a stable town. The processes of the community move toward a stable equilibrium. I well remember one of the criteria I had when I was looking for a town in which to practice medicine and to write. I had to have a well-defined community that had a sense of history and little prospect for development. In that environment I could create, not only my writing, but also my work—performing my work as I saw fit. Whether or not Union poises itself to lose its stability through growth is another question.

Approaching my work as I have, am I an exception in Union? I don't think so. I believe I am on firm ground in saying that the people I interviewed believe that they want to live in this community so they can do the work that they want, in the way they want, in a particular lifestyle that they seek and to raise their families with minimum worry. The community provided the stability to allow such creativity. Yes, I call it creativity. These people are not living a fad, nor are they paging through glamour magazines lusting after more and more things. They each have the courage to live in this town and forge a life that they consider worthwhile, even though it may not always pay off in money terms.

We see our surroundings upon the solid shoulders of others, upon the cultures of thousands of years, and from that vantage point, that solid foundation, we can see to create much as the eye sees at the top of the pyramid pictured on the back of our own dollar bill. What do we see? We each see something different. How can we see something that we might not have a word to describe? How can we describe a feeling we have never felt? How can we think something if we have no words for it? We can't. That's the essence of creativity, and it is the power for our continued existence—and possible destruction.

Within the group of people presented in these pages exists something, mostly indescribable, that flows through us from our ancestral past. It is a sense and longing for freedom, and this feeling bases itself more on Native American traditions than European traditions. The American Indian has embodied freedom to us, and in many ways, the American Indian personality was the one copied by early American westerners in the personification of the American cowboy.

In the first chapter of this book I said that Union is essentially uniform racially with few exceptions (our family being one of the exceptions), but that is not quite accurate. What is more accurate is that American Indian blood mixes with the blood of native Mainers throughout the state and with Americans throughout the country. The American Indian is here, though barely anyone sees it, nor does anyone talk about it. The American Indian tradition lives in us by what we mean by freedom, which is a freedom beyond what the early European immigrants had in mind. The people in this book have made sacrifices for a freer, more self-determined way of life even though we have forgotten, or ignored, the Indian influence (read about this idea in Robert Persig's book, *Lila*). The same can be said about the African influence in our nation, most obviously true with the music we love. That music originated from a longing for freedom.

A community must change with the times or die. It builds on the old, but merely bulldozing the old and replacing it with new, as is done in California, is not a satisfactory answer—at least not to me. Those who choose to live and work in a town allow the town to slowly evolve, which is a process much different from living in a place and allowing a Wal-Mart to enter the community thereby displacing smaller businesses that once provided those same services. That's on the scale of unholstering a gun, when the opponent has only bare knuckles.

To decide to work in town is a decision that says such individuals are ready to contribute to the worth of the town, and they will succeed if they stay in tune with the rhythms of the town, much as Gary Sukeforth, the owner of the Common Market (Chapter 4), has shown in his work and thought. A town cannot have a soul unless it has a center, a center that reflects its soul. What is the soul of a town? I cannot say. Some things need to remain a bit mysterious, and the best I can say is that it would be a set of ideas upon which the town was created and then reaffirmed through ensuing years. The name of the town can be a clue. We have a clue, therefore, in Union.

So, a center is important. Smallness is important. Does that mean that an individual can only find happiness in a small town? Hardly. Many people like the diversity and stimulation of a city. Regardless, they *have* to live somewhere. They will have friends and family. They will need to buy food somewhere and do the everyday activities to keep their lives going. The kids have to go to school. A small community forms around those needs, for each of us. The trick is to have a focal center to the community that somehow embodies these needs and gives the community a sense of continuity, usually with references to history. In Union, it is obviously the Common.

A community needs safety. In smallness, anonymity is lost; actions and deeds expose themselves for all to see. Smaller units lend to a safer environment. As Buddy Savage (the wine maker in Chapter 8) points outs, you cannot get away with much in a small community. Responsibility for your actions ever hovers above your head.

The people who choose to live and work within a community do not have it easy. Work becomes more of a journey of life-art than money generation. In many cases, a spouse must earn money elsewhere to support the farm or the household. Husband and wife can work together in a business and make it—sometimes—but not every husband and wife can work together. Herb and Vicki Harriman (on the horse farm in Chapter 15) remain a common paradigm with Vicki working as a nurse at a hospital and Herb trying to make the sawmill a successful endeavor. In my own life, I have been able to live and work in Union along with my wife, but only because, as a physician, I receive relatively more money per unit of work than the average worker, and we carefully watch our spending. Alan Heath (at the local plumbing and heating company in Chapter 10), works with his wife, Genie, and they do okay, but it is a lot of work. Individuals wanting to live and work in a one community have to know that they will probably never get rich, if that goal has any importance to them.

We live in a modernist world in America. It is consumer-driven, and living in the middle of it, we cannot always gauge ourselves. The message, "buy, buy, buy," surrounds us. The time we now have available, because of all the labor saving devices that we have invented, the time we once spent working, we now use in buying. Think about your time. Think about what you do with it. Think of the last family outing. Was it to the mall, or something similar? I'm not downgrading any of this. It is simply fact: we are a consumer-driven culture.

Though the people interviewed for this book do not have it easy, they refuse to live any other way. They remain accepting of the compromises and sacrifices required to support their chosen ways. As a lifestyle choice, it is not just a matter of choosing to live in the country or in a small community, it is choosing to both live and work within the community. These people speak to everyone considering working close to home. Anyone choosing to do so will likely make the same compromise of lifestyle over income, a decision that accentuates the bipolarities of life.

As retro as Union may appear to the casual observer, it maintains those elements necessary for a continuing and coherent community and serves as a model for community. That is not to suggest Union is unique in Maine in that respect. If Union loses the ability to tax its own citizens and make its own decisions regarding community structure, then in the future, it will likely become nothing more than a bedroom community. As such, I would never have chosen to live here. A particular identity remains important to a sense of community. Pride in community goes along with that.

◆   ◆   ◆

There exist just so many ways that people can live together in peace and harmony. These standards might be called "religious" standards. Religion does not form the heart of communities much any more, and perhaps that is a good thing. I make such an observation based on what I learned writing my last book, *Personality and the Soul: Sixteen Women Show Us the Connection*. That is to say, women form the matrix of a community in an informal way through communication and expression of particularly fine qualities, and these qualities help to hold the community together.

If I were to put these same women in a room leaving them to talk amongst themselves about these fine qualities and their origin, they would leave that room arm in arm. However, if I instructed them to discuss organized religion, I have no doubt that they would argue heatedly in short order, which says more about the topic than it does about these women. Organized religion cannot remain at the heart of any community unless nearly all the people in the community subscribe to that religion. Religion and religious values are one thing. Organized religion is another. I'll leave that subject to your own conjectures.

The positive qualities of honesty, integrity, courage, dedication, etc., are gold to a community. The women, with their better-refined communication skills, constitute a matrix for the community. Those people who both work and live in the community form important centers within that matrix. A relatively few centers within that matrix stand out, and I have labeled those the "truth outposts," though I have not described all that exist in Union.

In an effort to encourage people to get along peacefully, schools now have the task of "teaching" diversity. Educators think that students need exposure to diverse opinions and ways of life so that the students will learn to respect and accept one another better. I do not take issue with that. However, the success of any community derives from those qualities that we all hold *in common*, in greater or lesser degrees. Moreover, any community knows about these qualities, because without a majority of the community's citizens practicing some semblance of them, the community will fail to cohere.

How much diversity does a small town unit like Union really allow? I could talk about lifestyle—and zoning (of which Union has a semblance), but I would rather use for an example something I know about particularly: racial diversity.

From my own viewpoint, cultures are diverse, but race is merely appearance. Our family is multi-racial. We have four children, all adopted as babies. Three are East Indian, the fourth is from Florida with Jamaican heritage. These children grew up in Union, a place nearly 100 percent Anglo, with the exception of mostly hidden Native American blood. Plop four babies that don't look like the rest into a small town culture, what happens?

Nothing much. First, realize that these children, in growing up in Union, attended preschool with other Union children. They played with the same toys, watched the same movies and attended the same local cultural activities. These children form part of the Union culture, only they look different.

Children being what children are, they notice differences in appearance. We have taught our children to educate rather than react, and other children accept the explanation that our children are adopted and that their racial heritage comes from another part of the world. After that, it is mostly forgotten. The important fact is that they are from Maine culture, and they fit in. It would be much more difficult if they had moved into the community from elsewhere at, say, the age of fourteen.

The Association of Black Social Workers has railed against adoptions of black children into white homes because they say it takes away from legitimate black culture and only makes a black child white. That may be true, and I would agree with them unless white children be allowed adoption by black families. There should be no difference.

At least in our family we have found that race makes no difference, but culture does make a difference (though I must say that traveling with a multi-racial family is one of the greatest experiences, ever). For the children and other residents of Union, it appears easier for them to accept others who look different if they fit into and come from their own culture. For the majority of people at this time, looking different, but acting the same, is a good first step in accepting diversity.

I remember standing in line at the grocery store on the Common years ago when the children were small. Still a baby, Hazel was in the cart in her car seat. A person in line with me asked where Hazel was from, and I replied India. The person exclaimed, "Oh, does that mean she'll speak with an accent?"

"Ayuh," I replied.

◆   ◆   ◆

My hope is that this book will give to the readers a sense of the important components of communities and allow them to look at their own communities perhaps in a different way. For those dissatisfied with their life and thinking of relocating, consider living close to work. Living close to work adds strength to the community, and it adds strength to family. The sacrifices are money, anonymity and usually a peer group at work. The choice of lifestyle over money does not mean that these individuals or families who have made that choice have any less talent or intelligence than commuters. In fact, they may be the brightest among us given the benefits of the lifestyle they have chosen in today's world. It is success, redefined.

Are the people who both work and live in Union dinosaurs, remnants of the past? I don't think so. If we are going to survive as a species, the way I see it, they must be harbingers of the future.

Bibliography

Best, Steven and Kellner, Douglas, *The Postmodern Turn*, N.Y., The Guilford Press, 1997.

Cahoone, Lawrence E., *The Dilemma of Modernity: Philosophy, Culture, and Anti-Culture*, N.Y., State University of New York Press, 1988.

Cahoone, Lawrence E., *The Ends of Philosophy*, N.Y., State University of New York Press, 1995.

Cahoone, Lawrence E., *From Modernism to Postmodernism*, Cambridge, Mass., Blackwell Publishers Inc., 1996.

Cocking, J. M., *Imagination : a study in the history of ideas* ; edited with an introduction by Penelope Murray, London, Routledge, 1991.

Durant, Will and Ariel, *The Lessons of History*, N.Y., Simon and Schuster, 1968.

Faludi, Susan, *Stiffed: The Betrayal of the American Man*, N.Y., Harper Collins, 1999.

Forster, E. M., *Aspects of the Novel*, Harcourt, Brace & World, Inc., N.Y., 1927.

Groce, Philip C., "Ideas", *Beacon*, N.Y., Lucis Trust, 1997.

Groce, Philip C., *Personality and the Soul: Sixteen Women Show Us the Connection*, Rockland, Maine, Seven Coin Press, 2001.

Kaplan, Robert D., *The Ends of the Earth*, N.Y., Vintage Books, 1997.

Kiefer, Christie W., *The Mantle of Maturity : A History of Ideas About Character Development*, Albany, State University of New York Press, c1988.

Laing, R. D., *The Politics of Experience*, N.Y., Ballantine, 1968.

Mui, Constance L., Murphy, Julien S., *Gender Struggles: Practical Approaches to Contemporary Feminism*, N.Y., Rowman and Littlefield Publishers, Inc., 2002.

Persig, Robert M., *Lila*, New York, Bantam Books, 1992.

Williams, Ben Ames, *Come Spring*, Boston, Houghton Mifflin, 1940.

Index

978-0-595-36567-8
0-595-36567-1